POCKET

GARDENING
GUIDES

HERBS

❖

DAVID SQUIRE

POCKET

GARDENING
GUIDES

HERBS

❖

DAVID SQUIRE

Illustrated by Vana Haggerty

TIGER BOOKS INTERNATIONAL
LONDON

Designed and conceived by

THE BRIDGEWATER BOOK COMPANY LTD

Art Directed by PETER BRIDGEWATER

Designed by TERRY JEAVONS

Illustrated by VANA HAGGERTY FLS

Edited by MARGOT RICHARDSON

CLB 3379

This edition published in 1994 by

TIGER BOOKS INTERNATIONAL PLC, London

© 1994 Colour Library Books Ltd,

Godalming, Surrey

Printed and bound in Singapore

ISBN 1-85501-382-7

CONTENTS

EARLY HERBALS

❖

IN MEDIEVAL times, masses of herbs and spices were used to help cloak the incipient decay in food, as well as adding flavour and excitement to what otherwise might have been dull and monotonous meals. Herbs that had been spread throughout Europe by the Romans were widely grown, especially in monasteries.

During the Dark Ages, the combined knowledge of Persian, Greek and Roman herbalists was nearly lost. Fortunately, manuscripts survived and in the sixth century a library of herbals at the Benedictine monastery at Monte Cassino, Italy, provided a reservoir of knowledge that later spread to other monasteries. It became a rule that every Benedictine monastery should have at least one monk with a knowledge of herbs and their cultivation.

PEPPER (Piper nigrum) *was an important spice, helping to enrich many meals and to cloak the decay all too frequently present in food.*

IN THE *Middle Ages, monasteries were the repositories of culinary and medicinal herbs. Here is a herb garden from Cherubino da Spaloti's* Fior de Virtu, *published in Venice in 1490.*

The earliest herbal in Anglo-Saxon appeared in about 1050 and was based on earlier Greek texts. Further early English manuscripts followed, as well as others in Europe, in French and Italian.

With the introduction of moveable type in Germany in 1440, a method was created that enabled many copies to be taken from a single image, eventually leading to less expensive books.

DOCTOR-BOTANISTS

In early times, botany and medicine were closely wed, doctors often having to prescribe from plants available to them. From the time of Dioscorides, a doctor born in Asia Minor in the first century AD, to about the time of the Swedish botanist Carl Linnaeus who, in 1727, enrolled as a

THE SPICE TRADE

The high cost of spices throughout the Middle Ages was due to the long, perilous route by which they travelled to Western Europe from India and the Spice Islands of Indonesia. In 1498, the Portuguese discoverer Vasco da Gama rounded the Cape of Good Hope and reached India, though it was not until 1522 that the first cargo of spices reached Amsterdam direct. For the next twenty-five years the Portuguese dominated the spice trade, until in 1605 the Dutch captured the Molucca Islands and attempted to dominate the trade, partly by destroying Nutmeg and Clove trees from all islands except Amboina (sometimes Ambon).

Nutmeg
(Myrystica
fragrans)

The Dutch monopoly was finally broken by the British in 1796.

DURING *the fifteenth century, when spices were costly, new ways to reach the Spice Islands were tried. In 1492, Christopher Columbus travelled west in search of India, but instead landed in the New World.*

medical student at the University of Uppsala, doctors were as much herbalists as physicians.

Herbalists during this period came from all over Europe: Italy, Germany, Belgium, France and England. Many of them are still well-known today and include the barber-surgeon John Gerard (1545–1612), herbalist and apothecary John Parkinson (1567–1650) and the apothecary Thomas Johnson who, in 1633, revised Gerard's herbal, sorting out some of the mistakes in it. However, perhaps the best-known is the seventeenth-century English physician and herbalist Nicholas Culpeper. In 1652

NICHOLAS CULPEPER
(1616–1654) wrote one of the best known herbals, offering remedies developed and used in his own medical practice.

he published *The English Physician*, which later became better known as his Herbal and contained many recipes developed for use in his own practice. In 1640 he had set up in London as an astrologer and physician, an approach that made him unpopular with orthodox doctors. He was also disliked and dismissed in a derisory manner by the royalist College of Physicians because he supported the parliamentarians. Indeed, he was seriously wounded in the chest during the English Civil War and died of consumption when thirty-eight. Culpeper's book became a manual of herbal medicine for housewives.

BOTANICAL GARDENS

❖

BEFORE the establishment of botanic gardens during the sixteenth century, monastic gardeners were gatherers and nurturers of plants. Many culinary herbs were cultivated, as well as medicinal ones, although at that time there was a belief that *all* plants were of use to man and that their medical value was indicated by their shape. For example, plants with heart-shaped leaves were assumed to be a remedy for heart conditions, whereas the roots of some orchids resemble testicles and were crushed and eaten in an attempt to encourage sexual activity.

EARLY BOTANIC GARDENS
More reasoned thinking began in the early sixteenth century and the first botanic garden was founded in Pisa, Italy in 1543, followed two years later by one in Padua and in Florence in 1550. Many others were founded and by the end of the following century there were botanic gardens in Germany, France, Holland, Sweden, England and Scotland.

Early botanic gardens in Southern Europe grew medicinal and culinary herbs native to warm areas, while later ones further north and in countries which were maritime powers gathered plants from a wider area due to traders returning with seeds and rare specimens. Also, plants were exchanged between botanic gardens. By the eighteenth century, the wealth of plants arriving at botanic gardens necessitated a more convenient and logical naming system. This was devised by the brilliant, world-famous botanist Carl Linnaeus.

EARLY botanical gardens were repositories for many plants, especially medicinal and culinary herbs. Leiden Botanic Garden in the Netherlands, founded in 1587, was famous for its wide range of plants, which it later distributed to other European gardens. The illustration shows the garden in 1610.

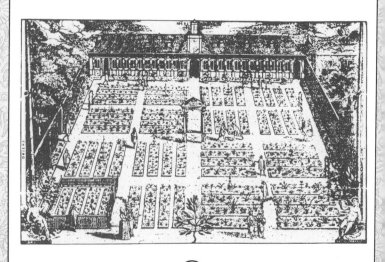

COOK BOOK TIME

Herbs to flavour foods have been used in most countries since early times and much about them recorded in herbals, although the interest was medicinal rather than culinary. It was not until the Renaissance in Italy during the fourteenth and fifteen centuries, and its spread across Europe in the sixteenth century, that the history of modern cookery began. From Italy – together with many cookery books – Catherine de Medici took this new culinary art to Paris, introducing a cultured simplicity previously unknown. The Italians also introduced forks and spoons to France, marking an epoch in the progress of dining and, consequently, cookery.

In England, many cookery books appeared in the sixteenth century, such as by Sir J. Elliott and Abraham Veale, while in

---

CARAWAY (Carum carvi) *has been a popular herb for several centuries and is seen here depicted in Pierandea Mattioli's* Commentaires *in 1579, orginally published in 1544 and firstly with illustrations in 1554.*

STREET CRIES FOR HERBS

Street pedlars, whether selling kebabs in Istanbul or water in Marrakech, have been plying their wares for centuries. In the Middle Ages, London became a hub of wandering pedlars and by the seventeenth century the lanes echoed with melodious cries.

Culinary and medicinal herbs were sold, but none more popular than lavender, with the cry:

'Who'll buy my lavender, fresh lavender. Sweet blooming lavender, who'll buy?'

1625 the *Widdowe's Treasure* was published and in 1665 Robert May wrote the *Accomplisht Cook*, which disparagingly referred to French cookery but highly of Italian and Spanish dishes. Hannah Woolley's cook book *Queen-like Closet* was published in London in 1670, but it was to be in the nineteenth century that the cook book phenomena became a mania. Eliza Acton's *Modern Cookery* was first published in 1845 and, with revisions, remained in print into the early twentieth century. But the cookery author above all others has been Mrs. Beeton. *Beeton's*, first issued in 1861, proved to be success, a landmark in publishing as well as the kitchen.

PLANNING A HERB GARDEN

 HERB gardens on a grand scale are always impressive, with dominant mounds of coloured sages perhaps overshadowed by large, umbrella-like flower heads of Angelica. But small is also beautiful and there are few gardens without space for two or three herbs, either in borders or containers on a patio or balcony.

The range of herbs is wide and includes annuals, biennials, herbaceous perennials, small shrubs and trees. Except for those with a woody nature, most die down during winter. Some, such as the well-known Parsley and Chervil, can be encouraged to grow outdoors through part or all of winter by placing cloches over them.

Herbs grow well in most soils that are freely drained and neither too acid nor too chalky. Because many herbs are native to warm climates, a sunny, wind-sheltered position is essential, especially to encourage early and late harvesting. Fertile, moisture-retentive soil encourages growth even during droughts. However, the herbs that are grown for their seeds do not need rich soil.

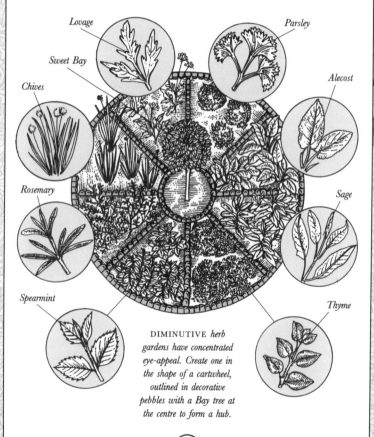

Lovage

Parsley

Sweet Bay

Alecost

Chives

Rosemary

Sage

Spearmint

Thyme

DIMINUTIVE *herb gardens have concentrated eye-appeal. Create one in the shape of a cartwheel, outlined in decorative pebbles with a Bay tree at the centre to form a hub.*

GAPS BETWEEN *natural stone paving create homes for low-growing herbs, such as the many thymes. More clinical settings are possible, such as formal paving slabs laid solely on a bed of sand, with gaps between them.*

BUYING HERBS

Many herbs can be raised from seeds (pages 52 and 53), others by cuttings (54 and 55) and a few by division (56 and 57). Alternatively, there is always the opportunity to buy young plants. Sources for these include nurseries, garden centres, high street shops and specialist mail-order companies.

If possible, inspect plants thoroughly before buying (mail-order ones on receipt). Reject those infested with pests and diseases, roots matted and coming out of the drainage hole, moss growing on the compost, and a generally neglected appearance. Poor plants never recover to develop into healthy, eye-catching specimens. If mail-order plants are not up to standard, immediately complain and contact the company.

HERBS IN CONTAINERS

Patio containers and window-boxes make herb growing possible for everyone, even flat-dwellers with only a balcony.

While Chives are handsome in pots, sages and mints in growing-bags and a medley of small herbs

PATIO CONTAINERS

Small, bushy herbs are ideal in containers on patios, where they create a wide array of leaf colours and textures. They can also be conveniently placed near kitchen doors to make them accessible during wet weather.

Window-boxes and troughs create good homes for mints, Marjoram, French Tarragon, Chives and thymes. Ideal on balconies.

Growing-bags support sages of all kinds, enabling the varied and attractively coloured leaves to contrast with each other (see page 57 for a few of them). Ornate pots are superb for thymes and Parsley. Planters with holes in their sides are excellent for Parsley and Chives.

in window-boxes and troughs, few are as imposing and eye-catching as a couple of Bay trees planted in large white tubs and positioned either side of a front door. They need regular clipping, but more than repay this time by their distinctive appearance.

CULINARY HERBS

❖

Herbs are some of the oldest cultivated plants we have and therefore their wide range, which includes annuals, biennials, herbaceous perennials, evergreen shrubs and trees, is not surprising. Some are grown for their leaves, which are used to flavour a wide range of dishes; others have seeds that introduce spicy flavours to foods and drinks. Roots and stems bring further flavourings.

Garnishing is another role of culinary herbs. Parsley is ideal for adding colour to sandwiches and as fish, while Spearmint, as well as being added to boiled potatoes and peas, also creates interest and colour when placed on cooked food in serving dishes on tables. Dill leaves are superb when garnishing boiled potatoes, peas and beans; they have also been used in salads. Chives are used either chopped or whole.

SOME *herbs are sown freshly from seeds each year. Parsley (left), really a biennial, is grown as an annual and sown either in pots or drills.*

Parsley

Bay

HORSERADISH *(left) is one of the few herbs grown for its long roots. When washed, crushed and prepared they create a well-known pungent, peppery condiment for use with meat, fish and salads.*

Horseradish

MOST *herbs are grown for their leaves. Some, such as the herbaceous Balm (below), have soft leaves that soon emit a pleasing bouquet when bruised, but the tree-like Bay (above) has tough leaves. Its leaves are an essential part of bouquet garni.*

Balm

Root section

CRYSTALLIZED STEMS

Angelica is widely grown for its stems which are cut, dried and crystallized with sugar, and used to flavour and decorate cakes and confectionaries. It has been grown commercially over a wide area, from Japan to France, including England, Moravia and Bohemia.

Angelica (Angelica archangelica) severed stem

SPICY *seeds play an essential role in many dishes, introducing exciting flavours. These herbs include Anise, Caraway, Coriander and Fennel. They are easily grown and harvesting them is simple. Storage needs only a few air-tight jars. Additionally, when growing in a herb garden they create an attractive array of finely-divided leaves and flower-heads.*

FLAVOURING BEERS AND SUMMER DRINKS

Brewing barley wine was probably one of the earliest industrial arts, and said to have been established in Egypt as early as 5000 BC. Indeed, an Egyptian papyrus records a barley-wine tax being collected in 3400 BC. The art spread to the Greeks, the Romans later acquiring it and taking it around Europe.

Later, in Northern Europe and North America, many beer-like, low-alcohol and undistilled beverages were made from plants then considered either medicinal or culinary herbs. Root beer was made from an infusion of herbs, barks and roots, including Wintergreen (*Gaultheria procumbens*) and Sarsaparilla (*Smilax*).

Beers have also been enhanced by herbs, such Alecost (*Chrysanthemum balsamita*), formerly known as Costmary. It emits a balsamic odour and is said to give ales a spicy taste.

Flavouring summer drinks is another role of herbs; Lemon Balm is frequently used, while some people use Spearmint, Peppermint or Applemint.

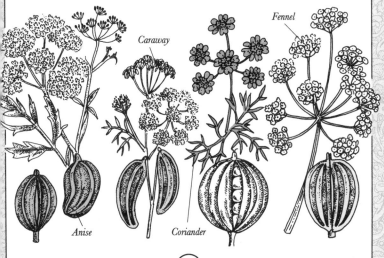

Fennel

Caraway

Anise

Coriander

FREEZING AND
DRYING HERBS
❖

ERBS are at their best when used fresh, but there are times during the year when this is impossible. Leaves of evergreen herbs, such as Rosemary and Bay, can be picked throughout the year, but even these are not at their best while in a semi-dormant state in winter. Also, it is possible to grow a few herbs in pots on a window sill indoors to extend their fresh season by a month or so, but to be assured of herbs throughout the year gathering and storing is an essential and interesting facet of growing culinary herbs.

Herbs can either be dried or frozen and although in these states they are not suitable as garnishes they are still superb for adding to food. Indeed, the flavour of many dried herbs is more concentrated than when fresh. Therefore only about half the amount is needed.

DRYING HERBS

There are two basic ways to dry herbs – in the air or by being placed in a gently-warm oven. The easiest and best method is by air, but both techniques are initially the same:

• Pick shoots and leaves while still young and before the plant develops flowers. Choose a warm, dry day, removing them in the morning before they feel the full sun.

• Discard aged, diseased or pest-damaged leaves.

• Tie young sprigs into small bunches. Avoid creating large clusters, as this reduces air circulation within them. Herbs with large leaves, such as sage, are best removed from their stalks and tied into small clusters.

• Frequently, blanching is recommended prior to drying and although it helps leaves to retain

FREEZING HERBS

This is an ideal way to produce herbs when fresh ones are not available. Ideally, they should be used within six months of being frozen. Leaves are harvested in a similar way as when air-drying them: young and fresh, before flower-heads are formed and picked early in the morning. Ideal herbs to freeze include tender-leaved types such as Sweet Basil, Chives, mint and Parsley.
There are two ways to freeze them, either whole or frozen in water.

• FREEZING WHOLE: *Select young, healthy shoots and leaves and place in plastic bags, firmly but not so that they are crushed. Seal each bag with a 'twist' and place in a firm, plastic box with a snap-type lid. Put in a freezer.*

• FREEZING IN WATER: *Select young, healthy leaves and chop them finely. Spread them in thin layers in ice-cube trays and fill with clean water.*
Place in a freezer. They can also be placed in the freezer part of a refrigerator. When solid, transfer to plastic freezer bags, label and seal.

FEATHERY and small-leaved herbs such as Chervil, Fennel and Marjoram can be tied in small bunches and hung upside down in an airy place. Avoid places where the atmosphere is damp, as this encourages diseases.

WHEN herbs are thoroughly dry, rub them gently between your hands and store them in airtight containers with screw-top lids. Ensure hands are dry before tackling this job, as otherwise leaves tend to stick to them.

FREEZING is a relatively recent way to keep herbs. Instead of placing in airtight containers, put measured amounts in ice-cube trays, add water and place in a freezer compartment. To use, just drop a cube in a dish.

colour, is not necessary. However, if you wish to do it, immerse the leaves in boiling water for a few seconds, shake to remove water and dry on clean, absorbent paper. Oven-dried herbs are usually blanched.

• Hang up the bunches in a well-ventilated, dry and fairly warm room to dry. Slow drying is better than rapidly in high temperatures, and usually takes five to twelve days. If the area is dusty, wrap the bunches in muslin or place in thin paper bags.

• Leaves and small sprigs are more easily dried by placing them on a tray. They then can be placed over a radiator, in an airing cupboard or even in a warming draw in an oven. Ensure they do not dry too rapidly: turn them every day. In this way, drying takes about three days.

• When oven-drying, place blanched herbs on a covered tray and put in an oven with the temperature at its lowest and the door ajar. Turn the leaves every twenty minutes – drying usually is complete within an hour. This is suitable for herbs such as sage, mint and Parsley that have been removed from their stalks.

• When leaves – whether air or oven-dried – are dry and crumbly, rub them between your hands. At the same time, remove stalks and mid-ribs. Place in airtight jars.

DRYING SEEDS

Some herbs, such as Anise, Coriander, Dill and Fennel, are grown for their seeds. These are gathered by cutting the flower-heads when fully ripe and hanging them upside down in an airy place. Either place a sheet of clean paper under them, or put in thin paper bags.

STORING HERBS

Store dried herbs in airtight jars in cool, dark cupboards. Avoid places above ovens, as hot, dry air may daily fluctuate the temperature. Also, select cupboards away from steamy cookers. If properly dried and stored, dried herbs will keep their flavour for about a year.

ANGELICA
Angelica archangelica

NATIVE to Northern Europe, Iceland, Greenland and Central Russia, this dominant, 1.8–3m/6–10ft tall, hardy biennial is a multi-purpose plant: young stems are candied, leaves added to fish dishes and roots used to flavour gin and liqueurs.

CULTIVATION

Also known as Archangel and Wild Parsnip, by nature it is a biennial, but by removing the flowers can be grown as a short-lived perennial.

Grow Angelica in fertile, moisture-retentive soil in full sun or light shade. Sow seeds thinly and evenly outdoors in seedbeds during late spring or early summer, in shallow drills about 30cm/12in apart. Germination takes two to three weeks and when seedlings are large enough to handle thin them 25–30cm/10–12in apart. Keep the seed-bed free from weeds and in early or mid-spring of the following year put the young plants into their permanent positions, setting them 75–90cm/2¹/₂–3ft apart.

If seeds and flower-heads are not wanted, cut them off when young to encourage plants to continue for another year. If seed heads are not removed, plants die down after flowering.

HARVESTING

When stems are grown to be candied, cut them off in early and mid-summer while still tender. Also, cut off all leaf stalks. Sideshoots can also be candied and these can still be removed in late summer.

Harvest leaves for using fresh or dried before plants flower.

USES

Greenish-white flowers

Thick, fleshy roots

Hollow stem

Stems are crystallized with sugar and used to flavour and decorate cakes and other confectionaries. Roots are used with juniper berries to flavour gin, while the seeds are employed in vermouth and chartreuse, as well as some muscatel wines. Leaves and roots are sometimes cooked with apples and rhubarb to reduce acidity, while leaves, when fresh, are frequently added to fish dishes and jams. Also used in *pot-pourri*.

Angelica was widely employed as a preventative against evil spirits and witchcraft, and used to counter spells and enchantment.

A N I S E E D
Pimpinella anisum

NATIVE to Southern Europe, Near East and Egypt, where it has been grown for many centuries, as well as now naturalized in Asia and North America. As a commercial crop it has been grown from South Russia to South America, including North Africa, Spain and Malta. Earlier it was widely grown in Greece and is mentioned by the Greek physician Dioscorides and the Roman writer and politician Pliny. In Roman times it was extensively cultivated in Tuscany.

Aniseed is a hardy annual, creating a dainty plant about 45cm/18in high and developing brilliant green, finely divided and toothed leaves and umbrella-like heads bearing small, white flowers during mid- and late summer.

CULTIVATION
Aniseed, also known as Anise, needs light, fertile, slightly alkaline soil and a warm, sheltered, sunny position to grow well.

Sow seeds evenly and thinly in 6mm/^{1}/$_4$in deep drills spaced 30cm/12in apart in mid-spring. Germination takes up to three weeks and, when seedlings are large enough to handle, thin them 20–30cm/8–12in apart.

Keep the soil weeded and well-watered during summer.

HARVESTING
Plants are ready to be harvested when the tips of the fruits have turned greyish-green. Hang plants in bundles in a warm, dry atmosphere, allow to dry, then thresh out the seeds.

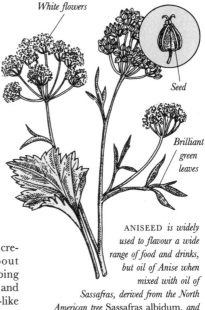

White flowers

Seed

Brilliant green leaves

ANISEED *is widely used to flavour a wide range of food and drinks, but oil of Anise when mixed with oil of Sassafras, derived from the North American tree* Sassafras albidum, *and Carbolic oil has been used to repel insects. Anise oil is also a good antiseptic and when mixed with oil of Peppermint or Wintergreen* (Gaultheria procumbens) *used to flavour toothpaste.*

USES
Seeds have for many centuries been used to flavour food and drinks such as Anisette, an aniseed-flavoured French liqueur. They are used in soups, cakes and sweets, as well as some cough mixtures. And when crushed they are sometimes sprinkled on meat to enhance its flavour.

The Roman poet Virgil, mentions Anise being used in spiced cakes and introduced at the end of meals to prevent indigestion. Such a cake was part of a marriage feast and thought to be the origin of spiced wedding cakes.

BALM
Melissa officinalis

Native to Central and Southern Europe, this bushy and branching plant has pale green, hairy, heart-shaped and nettle-like leaves that when bruised reveal a refreshing lemon bouquet. They are ideal for flavouring iced drinks and salads. During early and mid-summer, small, tubular, white flowers appear in clusters from leaf-joints.

Hairy leaves

White flowers

MEDICINALLY, *leaves are infused to make Balm tea, a refreshing drink for invalids. This is made by pouring 580ml/1 pint of boiling water on 28g/1oz of fresh leaves and leaving to infuse for twenty minutes. Then allow to cool. Longevity is a claim for Balm tea: one man who lived to 116 years breakfasted for fifty years on it sweetened with honey. Carmelite water, of which Balm was an ingredient, was taken daily by Charles V, the Holy Roman Emperor from 1519–56.*

CULTIVATION

Also known as Lemon Balm and Sweet Balm, this hardy herbaceous perennial grows 60–1.2m/2–4ft high and is ideal for planting in borders or herb gardens. Plant it in well-drained soil in full sun or light shade.

It is easily increased by lifting and dividing congested clumps every two or three years in autumn or spring. Replant young pieces from around the outside of the clump, setting them 38–45cm/ 15–18in apart. Alternatively, sow seeds outdoors in 6mm/1/4in deep drills during mid- and late spring. Germination takes two to three weeks and, when the seedlings are large enough to handle, move them to their permanent positions, setting them 38cm/15in apart.

In autumn or early winter, cut back all stems to ground level. In cold, exposed areas cover them with straw as protection against very low temperatures.

HARVESTING

Pick young leaves for use fresh during summer. Leaves can also be picked and dried, but this is best done before the plant begins to develop flowers.

USES

The refreshing nature of the leaves makes them ideal for both culinary and medicinal uses, as well as in perfumery. Balm was used in making *Eau des Carmes*, now displaced by *Eau de Cologne*, a distinctively-scented toilet water.

In food, it brings a refreshing lemon flavour to iced drinks in summer, also to fruit salads. Additionally, it introduces further flavour to chicken and fish dishes. Dried leaves retain their fragrance and therefore are ingredients for many types of *pot-pourri*.

SWEET BASIL
Ocimum basilicum

NATIVE to Tropical Asia, Sweet Basil is a tender annual with four-sided stems and aromatic, shiny green leaves with purple tinged grey-green undersides. They have a strong, clovelike bouquet and are highly valued for use in kitchens, especially with Italian tomato dishes. Plants grow about 45cm/18in high, and during mid- and late summer small, white flowers develop from leaf joints. They are borne in whorls.

CULTIVATION
This is a half-hardy annual and therefore fresh plants are raised each year. Choose well-drained, light soil and a sheltered, warm position in full sun. During late spring, form 6mm/¼in deep drills spaced 38cm/15in apart and sow seeds thinly and evenly. Germination takes two to three weeks. When large enough to handle, thin the seedlings 30–38cm/12–15in apart.

Plants can also be raised by sowing seeds 6mm/¼in deep in seed compost in pots or seed-trays during early spring and placing in 13°C/55°F. When large enough to handle, prick off the seedlings into individual pots, slowly acclimatize to outdoor conditions and plant into herb gardens when all risk of frost has passed. Space them 30–38cm/12–15in apart. Nip out the growing tips of plants to encourage bushiness.

HARVESTING
Pick leaves to use fresh throughout summer. Leaves can also be dried or frozen.

USES
Sweet Basil is a central ingredient of Italian tomato dishes and in pesto, a herb-based Italian flavouring used with pasta. Leaves are used fresh or dried to add flavour to omelettes, salads, soups, ragoûts, fish dishes and minced meat.

SWEET BASIL *has been cultivated in Morocco and Réunion, an island east of Madagascar in the Indian Ocean – both countries strongly influenced by France – for an essential oil used in perfumery, soap-making and to flavour liqueurs. In Mediterranean regions, the seeds of Sweet Basil were used to make a drink known as* Sherbet Tokhum, *a fizzy drink with a clove-like flavour.*

Soft leaves

IN FRANCE, *Sweet Basil is an ingredient of turtle soup, while in England it was used in the once famous Fetter Lane sausages of London.*

BAY
Laurus nobilis

WELL-KNOWN evergreen shrub native to the Mediterranean region and capable of growing 4.5m/15ft high. Usually, however, it is pruned and kept to half or less of that height.

The aromatic, glossy, mid- to dark green leaves are used to flavour cooked meals. During late spring, Bay bears inconspicuous greenish- yellow flowers.

CULTIVATION
Also known as Sweet Bay and Bay Laurel, it prefers well-drained, light soil and a sheltered position in full sun or light shade. A warm position is preferable as in cold, wind-exposed areas its leaves are often damaged. Therefore, in extremely cold areas grow Bay in a tub and move into a cool entrance porch or frost-proof shed during cold periods.

Increase Bay during mid- and late summer by taking 10cm/4in long sideshoots, trimming their bases and removing lower leaves. Insert them 3.6–5cm/1½–2in deep in equal parts moist peat and sharp sand. Place in a cold greenhouse or garden frame and, when rooted, move into individual pots. When established, plant into a garden or large tub.

Regular pruning is not normally needed, but container-grown plants need trimming two or three times during summer.

HARVESTING
Pick young leaves as required. If pot-grown plants are taken into porches during winter, leaves can be used fresh, but avoid spoiling the plant's shape. When young and newly picked, leaves are slightly bitter, but become sweet as they dry. When drying them, place in the dark to ensure their rich colours are retained.

USES
Leaves are an essential ingredient of *bouquet garni* and used in many pâtés and savoury dishes, including minced meat.

Woody stems

Evergreen leaves

BAY HAS *gained many usual common names from its wide range of uses. In France it is known as Laurier du Jambon (Ham Laurel) and in England as Fish Tree from its use in earlier days in pickling pilchards and sardines. It is also suitable for planting in tubs, where invariably it is encouraged to develop a trunk up to 1.2m/4ft high. Often grown in tubs outside restaurants.*

BORAGE
Borago officinalis

THIS annual, native to Europe, has for centuries been used as a culinary and medicinal herb. Indeed, it is said that Homer – a Greek poet in the eighth century before the birth of Christ – gained relief from grief by mixing the juice of Borage with wine: it was his *nepenthes*, a potion to bring him absolute forgetfulness.

Plants grow 45–90cm/1¹/₂–3ft high, have hollow stems and somewhat oval, green leaves covered with silvery hairs. From early to late summer it bears clustered heads of five-petalled, blue flowers. There are also white and pink flowered forms.

Blue flowers

Soft, hairy leaves

CULTIVATION
Borage is a hardy annual and therefore fresh plants are raised each year. Sow seeds evenly and thinly in shallow drills 30cm/12in apart from mid-spring to mid-summer, at four- to six-week intervals. Germination takes two to three weeks. When seedlings are large enough to handle, thin them 25–38cm/10–15in apart. Plants grow rapidly and leaves are ready to use within eight weeks.

HARVESTING
Pick and use leaves while young and fresh. Young leaves can be

THE FAME *of this fresh-looking herb extends beyond the improving of food and drinks. The sixteenth-century English barber-surgeon and enthusiastic botanist John Gerard said: 'Sprigs of Borage are of known virtue to revive the hypochondriac and cheer the hard student'.*

dried, but it is not easy: if ventilation is poor or the temperature too high they quickly turn black.

USES
Add young leaves to salads and fruit cups, where they introduce a fresh, cucumber-like flavour. Two or three leaves in a jug of fruit cup imparts a distinctive coolness. Indeed, one of its earlier names is Cool-tankard. The sweet-tasting flowers can be candied for sweets and cake decoration. Leaves and stems are frequently used in flower arrangements.

FRENCH FACTOR

French herbalists have used the leaves of Borage to combat fevers, colds and lung complaints, such as pneumonia and bronchitis.

CARAWAY
Carum carvi

NATIVE to a wide area, from the Mediterranean to Himalayas, Caraway is extremely popular for flavouring food as well as liqueurs. It is a biennial, with seeds sown once a year to produce plants up to 75cm/2¹/₂ft high during the following season and developing flower heads that later produce the desired seeds.

CULTIVATION
Sow seeds thinly and evenly in shallow drills spaced 30–38cm/ 12–15in apart in fertile, well-drained soil during late summer. Choose a sheltered, sunny position. When the seedlings are large enough to handle, thin them first to 15cm/6in apart, later 30cm/ 12in. Because Caraway is grown entirely for its seeds, there is no need to feed it.

During the second year, Caraway grows vigorously and develops fern-like, mid-green leaves. Small, green flowers appear in umbrella-like heads during mid-summer, followed by seeds.

HARVESTING
As soon as the seeds ripen, cut down the entire plant to ground-level. Tie the flower stems into small bundles and hang upside-down in a cool, dry, airy place until the seed-heads are dry – indicated by them falling off. At this stage, it is essential either to place paper bags over them or position a large piece of paper underneath.

Gather the seeds and put them through a fine sieve to separate fine, dust-like material.

USES
Dried Caraway seeds are used to flavour buns, cakes and bread, as well as salads and cheese dishes. Meats such as lamb and pork when roasted can be given a distinctive taste by using the seeds. Cabbage dishes also benefit from them, as well as sausages.

Seeds are also used to flavour the colourless German liqueur Kümmel, while Oil of Caraway is distilled from the fruits and widely used as a flavouring agent.

Green flowers

Fern-like leaves

Seeds

SEVERAL *superstitions surround Caraway: it was said to create unity and to keep lovers together. It therefore often formed part of love potions. The seeds were also said to prevent pigeons from straying! The thick, edible roots were acclaimed by John Parkinson, a gardener and herbalist, and said to have a flavour better than parsnips.*

CHERVIL
Anthriscus cerefolium

A HARDY biennial, native to south-eastern Europe and western Asia. Additionally, it is naturalized in North America, New Zealand and Australia. Chervil reaches 30–45cm/12–18in high and is grown for its bright green, fern-like leaves that resemble those of Parsley and used to garnish foods, introducing a delicate aniseed flavour. Its ridged stems are hollow and also aromatic.

White flowers

Bright green leaves

Bright green

Seed head

CHERVIL *has been used as a herb for several hundred years. At one time, scarcely a soup or salad did not have Chervil in it, which was frequently preferred to Parsley as a seasoner.*

HARVESTING
Use leaves when young and fresh, as these have the best flavour. Leaves can be dried or frozen, but cut them when young.

CULTIVATION
Although biennial by nature, Chervil is invariably grown as an annual and sown outdoors where it will grow and mature. It grows in most soils, preferably well drained, in full sun or light shade.

From late spring to mid-summer, sow seeds in shallow drills 30cm/12in apart. Germination takes two to three weeks and, when the seedlings are large enough to handle, thin them first to 15cm/6in apart, later 30cm/12in. Sow seeds at four-week intervals: plants develop leaves ready for cutting within eight weeks of being sown, but remember to pinch out all flower buds if seeds are not wanted. Water plants freely during dry periods to prevent flower stems.

USES
Garnishing salads and sandwiches, as well as flavouring soups, egg and fish dishes and sauces. It is also used as *fines herbes* for omelettes. Dried leaves are frequently used in stuffings.

Sweet Cicely (Myrrhis odorata) *is often confused with Chervil as it is also known as Great Chervil, Sweet Chervil and Cow Chervil. The anise flavoured leaves of Sweet Cicely were used in salads, the stems and roots boiled as vegetables.*

It also had a medicinal use, the roots being used to counteract bites from vipers and mad dogs!

23

CHIVES
Allium schoenoprasum

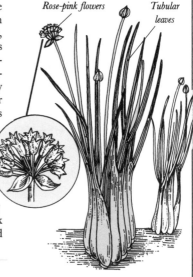

Rose-pink flowers

Tubular leaves

N ATIVE to a wide area in the northern hemisphere, from northern and southern Europe, through northern Asia to Japan as well as North America. This grass-like, onion-flavoured hardy perennial has been grown for many centuries to garnish and flavour food. Although mainly known as Chives, in North America it is also called Cive – a derivative of the French *civette* – and Schnittlaugh.

Plants, usually 15–25cm/ 6–10in high, are formed of tubular, mid-green leaves. During early and mid-summer, rose-pink flowers appear in dense, rounded heads at the tops of long stems.

CHIVES *are superb as a garnish or in soups, but have also been used in home-made sausages, croquettes and beefsteak puddings and pies. Not so flattering: chopped Chives were mixed with food and fed to newly hatched turkeys.*

CULTIVATION
Chives form clumps and after three or four years are best lifted, divided and young parts from around the outside replanted about 30cm/12in apart in light or moderately heavy well-drained soil in full sun or light shade.

Plants can also be raised from seeds sown in 12mm/^{1}/$_2$in deep drills spaced 30cm/12in apart in spring or early summer. Germination takes two to three weeks. When seedlings are large enough to handle, thin them to 15cm/6in apart. Later, transplant them to their permanent positions, 30cm/12in apart.

Keep plants well watered in summer and remove flower stems to encourage the development of leaves. Plants die down in autumn and develop fresh shoots in spring. Chives can also be grown in small containers and window-boxes; in autumn pots taken indoors and put on cool window sills provide leaves until mid-winter.

HARVESTING
Cut off leaves close to their bases and use fresh. Regular cutting encourages the development of further leaves. They can also be dried or frozen.

USES
The mild onion flavour of the leaves makes them ideal for flavouring sandwiches, soups, omelettes, egg and cheese dishes. They are also used as *fines herbes* and in *sauce tartare*.

Chives can also be finely chopped and added as a garnish to mashed potatoes, as well as being boiled with fresh new ones.

CORIANDER
Coriandrum sativum

THIS native of southern Europe and Asia Minor has spread throughout many parts of the world. It has an annual nature, erect and 23–75cm/9–30in high, with dark green, somewhat feathery, fern-like leaves and pink-mauve flowers during mid-summer. These develop seeds which are used to flavour food. The leaves are also used as flavourings in some dishes.

CULTIVATION
It is a hardy annual and fresh plants are raised each year. Sow seeds thinly and evenly in shallow drills 30cm/12in apart during mid-spring. Germination takes two to three weeks and, when seedlings are large enough to handle, thin them to 15cm/6in apart. Plants flower in early summer and seeds ripen during mid- and late summer. It grows in most soils and is especially suitable for sowing in land well manured during the previous year. Do not sow in land where manure has been dug in during the year seeds are sown, as this encourages lush, rank growth that delays the development of flowers and seeds. A sunny, open position is essential to encourage rapid ripening.

HARVESTING
Commercially, seeds are harvested when about two-thirds of the fruits have turned from green to grey. In a home garden, however, they can be left slightly later. Stems are cut and the seed-heads dried under cover. Rub out the seeds and store them either whole or ground into a powder.

By the way, unripe green seeds, as well as the leaves, have a strange, bug-like odour, but this changes and is replaced by a pleasant, sweet, aromatic bouquet.

USES
The feathery leaves are used to add a spicy flavour to soups and meat dishes, while seeds are added crushed or whole to curries and stews. They are also introduced to some liqueurs, as well as used in perfumery and the manufacture of soap.

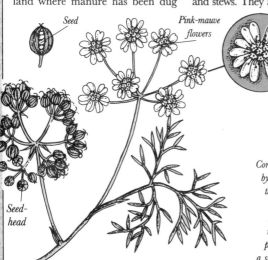

Seed

Pink-mauve flowers

Seed-head

LIKE *many other herbs, Coriander was widely spread by the Romans, and during the century before the birth of Christ was used by Hippocrates, the father of medicine, and other Greek physicians. It was used as a stimulant and carminative.*

DILL
Anethum graveolens

NATIVE to a wide area, from southern Europe to India and naturalized in North America and the West Indies. It grows 60–90cm/ 2–3ft high, with upright, hollow, ridged stems and blue-green, feathery, thread-like, anise-flavoured leaves. From early to mid-summer it develops small, star-like, yellow flowers borne in umbrella-like heads up to 7.5cm/3in wide. Both the seeds and leaves have culinary uses.

Incidentally, do not grow Dill and Fennel close together as it is then difficult to identify the self-sown seedlings.

Yellow flowers

Seeds

Seed-head

Blue-green leaves

IN THE *Middle Ages in Europe, Dill was frequently used by magicians in spells and charms against witchcraft. In addition to its culinary value, an oil distilled from the plant is used medicinally as a stimulant and carminative to expel gases from stomachs and intestines.*

CULTIVATION
Dill is a hardy annual and grows in well-drained, fertile soil and a sunny position. Sow seeds thinly and evenly 12mm/1/2in deep in drills, at four-week intervals, from early spring to mid-summer. Space the drills about 30cm/12in apart. Germination takes ten to fourteen days and when seedlings are large enough to handle, thin them to 23–30cm/9–12in apart.

Keep the plants well watered to encourage rapid growth. Seeds that fall on soil soon germinate.

NORSE WORD

The derivation of the word Dill is varied: Prior's Popular Names of English Plants *suggests it originates from the old Norse word* dilla *meaning 'to lull', referring to the plant's carminative qualities.*

HARVESTING
Pick and use the leaves fresh, as they are rather difficult to dry: they do not retain a bright, healthy colour. Instead of using leaves in winter it is better to use seeds which have been dried and stored in airtight jars. When growing plants mainly to produce seeds, cut down stems when the seeds turn brown in late summer.

USES
Use fresh leaves to garnish and flavour salads, fish, boiled potatoes, peas, beans, soups and poultry. Seeds have a stronger anise flavour and are often added to vinegar when pickling gherkins.

FENNEL
Foeniculum vulgare

DISTINCTIVE and handsome perennial, native to Europe, growing 1.5–2.4m/5–8ft high and developing thread-like, blue-green leaves and umbrella-like heads up to 10cm/4in wide packed with golden-yellow flowers during mid- and late summer. Its leaves are used to flavour food, while the strongly anise-flavoured seeds are used in bread, cakes and soups.

CULTIVATION
Fennel needs fertile, well-drained soil and a sunny position. Sow seeds of this hardy herbaceous perennial evenly and thinly in late spring or early summer in shallow drills spaced 38–45cm/15–18in apart. If seeds are needed, it is best to sow them in early spring.

Germination is not rapid, but when the seedlings are large enough to handle, thin them to 30–38cm/12–15in apart. Alternatively, lift and divide congested plants in spring, as soon as shoots appear. Replant young pieces from around the outside, setting them 38–45cm/15–18in apart. Unless seeds are needed, pinch off all flower buds to prevent their unnecessary development.

HARVESTING
Use leaves fresh during summer. Leaves are difficult to dry satisfactorily. However, they can be gathered in early and mid-summer and frozen.

To produce seeds, do not remove the flower buds and gather the seeds in late summer or early autumn, just before they are fully ripe. Spread the seed-heads on white paper and allow to dry slowly and without artificial heat. Ensure there is a flow of fresh air over them to prevent the development of fungal growths. Turn the seed-heads daily and when all the seeds have separated store them in airtight jars in a cool cupboard.

USES
Leaves are used to flavour fish and cheese dishes, vegetables, sauces, chutneys and pickles, while the seeds bring added flavour to bread, cakes and soups.

IN MEDIEVAL *times, Fennel was frequently used, together with St. John's Wort, as a preventive against witchcraft and other evil influences. It was also mentioned in Anglo-Saxon cookery and medical recipes.*

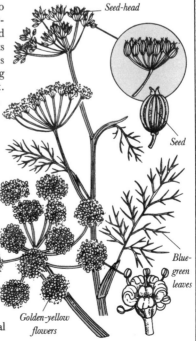

Seed-head

Seed

Blue-green leaves

Golden-yellow flowers

HORSERADISH
Armoracia rusticana

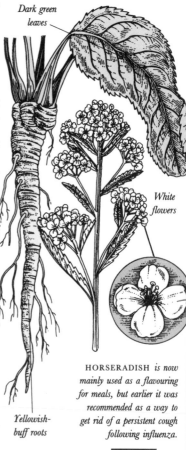

Dark green leaves

White flowers

Yellowish-buff roots

HORSERADISH *is now mainly used as a flavouring for meals, but earlier it was recommended as a way to get rid of a persistent cough following influenza.*

NATIVE to a wide part of Europe, western Asia and the Mediterranean region, Horseradish was widely used in the Middle Ages in Europe as a universal medicine. It has even been used mixed with vinegar to remove freckles, but since about the seventeenth century has been widely acclaimed as a condiment.

Plants reach about 60cm/2ft high and bear rough-surfaced, wavy-edged or lobed, dark green leaves about 45cm/18in long. Small, white, four-petalled flowers appear in early summer, but it is the long, yellowish-buff tap-roots that are the reason for growing it. They have a pungent, peppery flavour.

CULTIVATION
Horseradish is a hardy perennial. It is also known as Mountain Radish, Red Cole and Great Raifort, and earlier as *Cochlearia armoracia*.

Deeply-cultivated, fertile, well-drained soil and full sun or light shade suit it. By nature, it is a perennial and can be left in position for many years, a few roots being dug up as needed in summer. However, it can also be grown as an annual crop and roots planted each year. In early winter, dig up plants, sever main roots and cut into 15–20cm/6–8in long pieces. Store in sand or peat until shoots develop in early spring. Then, use a dibber to plant them 45cm/18in apart and with their tops 5cm/2in below the surface. Firm soil around them and water thoroughly. During late spring and summer the roots develop foliage which is cut down to soil level in early autumn.

HARVESTING
In autumn, dig up the roots and either use immediately or store in sand or peat.

USES
Roots are washed then crushed, grated or minced and simmered with milk, vinegar and seasoning. This peppery-flavoured condiment is used with meat, fish and salads, as well as for flavouring sauces. It is most widely used with beef.

HYSSOP
Hyssopus officinalis

THIS hardy, partially ever-green perennial is native to a wide area, from Mediterranean regions to Central Europe. It is grown for its young leaves that have a mint-like flavour, and used fresh in a wide range of foods, or dried and mixed in stuffings.

Plants grow 45–60cm/1¹/₂–2ft high, bushy and with aromatic, narrow, mid-green leaves on upright, branching stems. From mid- to late summer, plants develop purple-blue, tubular flowers.

CULTIVATION
Plant it in light, well-drained soil in full sun or light shade. It can be increased in several ways: sow seeds evenly and thinly in a seed-bed during mid- and late spring in 6mm/¹/₄in deep drills spaced 30cm/12in apart. Germination takes between two and three weeks and when seedlings are large enough to handle, thin them 15cm/6in apart. In late summer or early autumn, plant into their permanent positions, around 30cm/1ft apart.

Alternatively, take 6.5–7.5cm/2¹/₂–3in cuttings in late spring and insert in equal parts moist peat and sharp sand. Place in a cold frame or cool greenhouse and when rooted, pot up into individual pots. Plant into a herb garden in late summer.

Plants usually need replacing every three or four years.

HARVESTING
Pick the bitter, minty leaves throughout the year and use fresh. However, they are said to be at their best just before the flowers open. Leaves can also be dried, but pick when young.

USES
Fresh leaves are put in salads, as well as fresh or dried in stuffings or soups. In cooked dishes they are used to 'balance' oily fish or fatty meats. When dried they are included in *pot-pourri*.

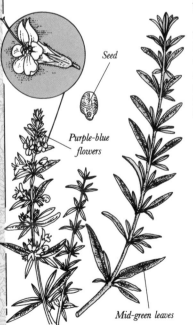

Seed

Purple-blue flowers

Mid-green leaves

HYSSOP *is sometimes grown for the oil from its leaves which is used to flavour liqueurs. Additionally, the flowers have been used to create a medicinal tea. A recipe in an old cookery book instructs: "Infuse a quarter of an ounce of dried hyssop flowers in a pint of boiling water for ten minutes; sweeten with honey and take a wineglassful three times a day, for debility of the chest."*

SWEET MARJORAM

Origanum majorana

NATIVE to southern Europe, this bushy, small, shrubby plant with four-sided, red stems and greyish, hairy leaves grows 30–45cm/12–18in high. And from early to late summer it bears clusters of tubular, white, pink or mauve flowers from grey-green, knot-like bracts, which gives rise to one of its common names. (Bract is a botanical name for a modified leaf).

Apart from culinary values it has been used medicinally against rheumatism and to soothe bruises.

CULTIVATION

Sweet Marjoram, also known as Knotted Marjoram and Annual Marjoram, is shrubby in its warm, native countries, but in northerly regions is unable to survive cold winters and therefore usually grown as an annual.

Sow seeds thinly and evenly in drills 6mm/¼in deep and 23–30cm/9–12in apart during mid- and late spring. When the seedlings are large enough to handle, thin them first to 15cm/6in apart, later 30cm/12in. Alternatively, to produce leaves earlier in the year, sow seeds in late winter or early spring, 3mm/⅛in deep in pots or seed-trays and place in 13–15°C/55–59°F. Prick out the seedlings when large enough to handle into small pots and plant into a herb border in late spring.

Set the plants in well-drained soil and a warm, sunny position.

HARVESTING

Pick leaves as needed, but preferably before plants flower. Leaves can be dried or frozen – cut the shoots slightly above soil level.

USES

Young shoots and leaves are used to create a sweet, spicy flavour in meat, poultry and game, as well as fish and tomato dishes. They can also be used in salads and are frequently added to soups, stews, stuffings, omelettes and pies. Leaves have a stronger flavour when dried and are frequently used in *pot-pourri*. Also, traditionally part of bunches of mixed herbs known as *bouquet garni*.

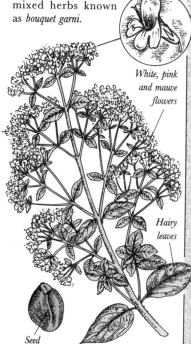

White, pink and mauve flowers

Hairy leaves

Seed

SWEET MARJORAM *is both a culinary and medicinal herb. It was effective against rheumatism if boiled in water and then drunk. It was also said to cure convulsions, cramps and toothache. Additionally, the leaves, when dried and mixed with honey, created a soothing and healing ointment for bruises and sores.*

SPEARMINT
Mentha spicata

NATIVE to Central Europe, this popular, aromatic, herbaceous herb has spread throughout much of the world and is famous for the sauce made from its leaves that is widely used to flavour lamb. It is most popular in English-speaking countries; infrequently used in France.

The leaves have a distinctive, spearmint-like aroma and taste which they readily transfer to sauces. Its upright shoots, which become slightly woody when old, grow 30–60cm/1–2ft high and with underground stems plants spread rapidly, becoming invasive.

CULTIVATION
It is easily grown in fertile, well-drained but moisture-retentive soil in a warm, sheltered position. Plants are easily increased by lifting and dividing congested clumps in spring and replanting young parts from around the outside. Alternatively, take 10–15cm/4–6in long cuttings of basal shoots in early summer and insert them either in equal parts sharp sand and moist peat, or directly into their growing positions if the soil is light and sandy. Plant about 30cm/12in apart and renew them every two or three years.

To prevent excessive spreading, either plant into a bottomless bucket buried to its rim in the ground, or a patio container.

HARVESTING
Pick leaves and use fresh throughout summer. Leaves can also be dried. For this, light soil produces the best plants. Leaves are rubbed through a sieve (with about twenty meshes to every 2.5cm/1in) and stored in a dry place. Leaves can also be cut off and frozen.

USES
Used to create sauces and jellies, mainly for flavouring lamb. They are also put in with cooking vegetables, such as potatoes and peas. Other preparations include mint vinegar and mint punch.

Pale blue flowers

Seed

Mid-green leaves

SPEARMINT *has acquired many other common names including Common Mint, Lamb Mint, Garden Mint, Mackerel Mint, Our Lady's Mint and Sage of Bethlehem. And in addition to its culinary values, medicinally it has been used to treat stomach complaints, and commercially in the preparation of toothpaste, chewing-gum and sweets. In addition to Spearmint, there are many others, including Apple Mint with rounded leaves. It is also used to make mint sauce.*

PARSLEY
Petroselinum crispum crispum

Small, yellow flowers

Bright green leaves

Seed-head

Seed

PARSLEY has been grown as a herb for several centuries. Native of Central and southern Europe, its distinctive, mildly spicy flavour makes it invaluable in sauces, salads and garnishes. Also, it contains generous amounts of vitamins A and C, as well as being extremely rich in iron compared to any other vegetable.

CULTIVATION
Parsley is a hardy biennial, but invariably grown as an annual. Sow seeds 6mm/1/4in deep in open ground from late winter to early summer. Choose well-drained, fertile soil and a sunny or lightly shaded position, setting the drills 20–25cm/8–10in apart. Germination is slow, but can be speeded up by watering the drill with boiling water before sowing.

When the seedlings are large enough to handle, thin them first to 7.5cm/3in apart, later 15–23cm/6–9in. Sowings can be made in greenhouses a month or so earlier, in 10–15°C/50–59°F, setting the plants 23cm/9in apart in gardens after slowly acclimatizing them to outdoor conditions.

THE GREEKS *held Parsley in great esteem, crowning victors of the pan-Hellenic Isthmian Games with chaplets of it. The Greeks also made wreaths of Parsley to adorn the tombs of their dead and therefore never employed its culinary virtues.*

In late summer, cut down plants and water thoroughly to encourage fresh growth. Cover young shoots with cloches.

HARVESTING
Pick leaves when plants are young to encourage the development of further leaves. For drying, gather leaves early in the day. Wash and dry rapidly in 93°C/200°F. Leaves can also be frozen.

USES
Widely used in sauces and salad dressings and as an essential ingredient of *bouquet garni*. It is also ideal for garnishing sandwiches.

PARSLEY PARADE

Its fame in kitchens is widely known, but the stems when dried and powdered have been used as a culinary colouring. While the roots have been used to create a tea, the French pounded green Parsley and snails in a mortar to form an ointment used to treat scrofula, now a rare condition but then known as King's evil.

ROSEMARY
Rosmarinus officinalis

ROSEMARY is steeped in history and has spread throughout the world from its native southern Europe and Asia Minor. It is famed for its scented flowers, while the aromatic, dark green leaves have a camphorous bouquet and, used fresh or dry, bring added flavour to food.

ROSEMARY abounds in history and literature. It became an emblem of fidelity for lovers and was frequently used in weddings. Anne of Cleves is said to have worn a wreath entwined with Rosemary at her wedding to Henry VIII in 1540, while branches, richly gilded and tied with silken ribbons, were presented to guests as symbols of loyalty and love.

CULTIVATION
Rosemary is an evergreen shrub, widely grown in shrub and herb borders. It is easily increased from 10cm/4in long cuttings in mid-summer: remove the lower leaves and insert in pots of equal parts moist peat and sharp sand. Preferably, place in a cold frame, but they root just as well in a sheltered corner on a patio. When rooted, pot up individually and plant into a border a year later.

Little pruning is needed, other than cutting out dead shoots in early spring and shortening straggly growths. Where old bushes are overgrown, cut them back by half in mid- or late spring.

HARVESTING
The leaves are used fresh or dried. When fresh, remove them from the plant as needed. When used dry, whole stems are cut and hung up, but there is a noticeable loss of flavour.

USES
In addition to its medicinal qualities – a decoction of Rosemary is said to help cure diseases of the head as well as easing aches in teeth and gums – leaves are used fresh or dried for flavouring food. It is frequently added to tomato soup, stews and, when finely chopped, to cooked peas. Additionally, the leaves are used to flavour roast meat and as an ingredient of sauces and stuffings. Use sparingly with lamb, pork, veal and chicken. Also used with fish.

Earlier, Rosemary had a reputation of strengthening the memory. Indeed, there is a saying 'Rosemary for Remembrance'.

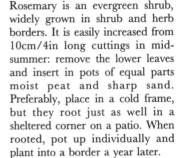

Mauve flowers

Aromatic leaves

Seed

Woody stem

RUE
Ruta graveolens

OFTEN known as Herb of Grace, Herb of Repentance and Herbygrass, this somewhat shrubby plant from southern Europe is widely grown both as a culinary herb and to decorate flower borders with its deeply divided, blue-green leaves. During early and mid-summer – and often into late summer – it bears clusters of 12mm/1/2in wide, sulphur-yellow flowers at the ends of young shoots. It is, however, the leaves, with their acrid odour and bitter flavour, that are used to add flavour to food.

CULTIVATION
Rue is a hardy, evergreen shrub, seldom more that 75cm/21/2ft high. When young, it forms neat, low, rounded hummocks that are ideal alongside border edges. Using garden shears to trim plants to within a few inches of the old wood in spring helps to keep them low and neatly shaped. In autumn, cut off dead flowers.

It is easily increased by taking 7.5–10cm/3–4in-long cuttings from sideshoots during mid-summer, and inserting them in equal parts moist peat and sharp sand. Place in a cool greenhouse – or on a north-facing window sill indoors – until rooted. Then, transfer into individual pots and overwinter in a cold garden frame. Alternatively, sow seeds 3–6mm/1/8–1/4in deep in seed drills in a seed-bed outdoors during spring. When the seedlings are large enough to handle, thin them 23–30cm/9–12in apart. Later, set them 45cm/18in apart in a border in late summer or autumn. Pinch out their growing tips to encourage bushiness.

HARVESTING
Pick young leaves, for use immediately or drying. When used fresh, chop finely. For a supply in winter, pick and dry fresh leaves, then store in airtight containers.

USES
Use chopped leaves sparingly in salads, remembering that they impart a bitter flavour.

Sulphur-yellow flowers

Blue-green leaves

Woody stem

Seed

RUE WAS *thought by the Greeks to have anti-magical qualities. It was used during the Middle Ages as a defence against witches. Earlier it was reported by Pliny, a Roman writer during the first century AD, that "Engravers, Carvers and Painters do ordinarily eat Rue alone to preserve their eye-sight".*

SAGE
Salvia officinalis

Violet-blue flowers

Grey-green leaves

Seed

THIS popular and widely used shrub from southern Europe has wrinkled, aromatic, grey-green and slightly bitter-tasting leaves that introduce added flavour to meals. There are purple and golden-leaved forms (see page 57), but these are mainly used decoratively.

CULTIVATION
Although hardy, sage is short-lived and usually replaced every three or four years. Also, plants tend to become straggly and with bare centres after a few years if not trimmed annually in late summer. Choose well-drained, light soil and a sunny, sheltered position. Raise plants by taking 7.5cm/3in long cuttings in late summer and inserting them in equal parts moist peat and sharp sand. Place in a cold greenhouse or frame. Pot up into individual pots when rooted and overwinter in a cold frame. Nip out the growing tips to encourage bushiness.

Sage can also be raised from seeds sown in early spring in pots of seed compost and placed in 16–18°C/61–64°F. Germination takes three to four weeks. When the seedlings are large enough to handle, transfer them to a nurserybed outdoors, setting them 15cm/6in apart. Later, when established, transplant them to about 38cm/15in apart into a herb border.

Alternatively, sow seeds 6mm/¼in deep in a seedbed outdoors in late spring. When large enough to handle, transfer the seedlings to 15cm/6in apart in a seedbed. Later in the year, plant them into their permanent positions in a herb garden.

LIKE MANY *other herbs, Sage was well known to the Romans who spread it throughout Europe. As well as flavouring foods, it has been used to clean teeth, and infused to make tea to strengthen gums and whiten teeth. Sage tea was very popular and highly prized by the Chinese who imported it from Holland.*

HARVESTING
Leaves are usually cut in bunches and used fresh or hung up and dried quickly in a warm room. Store them in airtight jars.

USES
Sage has many culinary values and is traditionally used with fatty meats such as duck, goose and pork. It is also used in stuffings as well as with cheese, veal, liver and onions. It is extensively used in Italian cooking.

SAVORY
Satureja

Lilac or rose-purple flowers

Seed

SAVORY *is an
ancient herb and
thought to have been
used before the East
Indian spices were
known. Indeed, vinegar
flavoured with Savory
was used by the Romans
in the same way as mint
is employed in
England today.*

Dark green leaves

Hairy stems

THERE are two types
of this ancient herb:
Summer Savory (*Satureja
hortensis*) and Winter
Savory (*Satureja montana*).

Summer Savory, native
to Europe, is a bushy
annual growing about
30cm/12in high and with
square, hairy stems and
dark green, strongly aro-
matic leaves. While
Winter Savory, originally
from Europe and Asia, is
perennial with an upright
but compact habit, 30cm/12in
high and woody, branching stems.

CULTIVATION

Although different in nature, these
two plants can be raised from seed
in the same way. During mid-
spring, form 6mm/¼in deep
drills 23cm/9in apart where they
are to grow. Choose a sunny position and fertile, well-drained soil.
Germination takes two to three
weeks and when large enough to
handle, thin the seedlings of
Summer Savory to 15–23cm/
6–9in apart, and those of Winter
Savory to 23–30cm/9–12in.

Seeds of Summer Savory are
sown each year, while the perennial Winter Savory needs replace-
ment every two or three years.

HARVESTING

Pick leaves throughout summer to
use while fresh. At flowering time
– from mid- to late summer – cut
down the plants and hang up
bunches to dry for winter use.

USES

The leaves and stems of Summer
Savory have a strong and spicy
flavour and can be added to soups
as well as meat and fish dishes,
stuffings and drinks. Also, they
may be used in *pot-pourri*.

In France, Summer Savory is
frequently used when cooking
broad beans, whereas in England
it is mint that is used. Winter
Savory is used in a similar manner, but the flavour is coarser.

AMERICAN FACTOR

*Savory must have been popular
in England in the early seventeenth century as about that time
it was taken by settlers to North
America. An early colonist, John
Josselyn, lists Savory among
plants taken there, while Bernard
McMahon in* McMahon's
American Gardener, *published in 1806, details its
cultivation. Incidentally, apart
from its culinary qualities, all
savories give instant relief when
rubbed on wasp and bee stings.*

FRENCH SORREL

Rumex scutatus

ALSO known as Garden Sorrel and Buckler-shaped Sorrel, French Sorrel is popular as a culinary herb.

CULTIVATION

French Sorrel is a slender, slightly prostrate European plant growing 30–45cm/12–18in high. Small, green to red flowers appear in clustered heads: they must be nipped out to encourage the growth of fresh leaves.

It is easily increased by lifting and dividing congested clumps in spring or late summer and replanting young, fresh pieces about 20cm/8in apart in rich, moist soil in full sun or light shade. Alternatively, sow seeds thinly and evenly 6mm/¼in deep in a seed-bed outdoors during mid-summer. When the seedlings are large enough to handle, transplant them to their permanent positions, about 20cm/8in apart.

HARVESTING

Cut off young leaves – which have a lemony flavour – when needed. Leaves are usually used fresh, but they can be dried or frozen in bags.

USES

Young leaves are added to sandwiches, salads and soups. Alternatively, older leaves can be cut and cooked like spinach. They can also be made into a purée and served with fish and rich meats.

In France they are formed into sorrel soup, as well as to flavour sauces and omelettes.

POPULAR WITH HENRY VIII

*Wild Sorrel (*Rumex acetosa*) is also used to flavour salads, but to many palates the leaves are too acid. Before the introduction of French Sorrel into Britain in about 1596, it was very popular and held in great repute by Henry VIII. It continued to be used, being mentioned in about 1720 by the garden writer and designer John Evelyn who wrote that it should never be omitted from salads. At one time, leaves were beaten into a mash and mixed with sugar and vinegar, creating a sauce for use with cold meat.*

Reddish-green flower

FRENCH
*Sorrel is a popular herb, especially in France where several forms were grown. Wild Sorrel (*Rumex acetosa*) is another type of sorrel and illustrated here. It has mid- to grey-green triangular leaves that form a thick clump. It is more upright than French Sorrel.*

Fleshy, mid-green leaves

FRENCH TARRAGON
Artemisia dracunculus 'Sativa'

ALSO known as True Tarragon, this widely-grown herb has leaves with a strong and sweet flavour, reminiscent of mint.

CULTIVATION

French Tarragon is a perennial shrub growing to about 60cm/2ft high and spreading by underground stems. The aromatic, narrow grey-green leaves cluster on upright stems. Small, white, globular flowers appear in loose clusters during mid-summer, but do not open fully in cool climates.

Tarragon thrives in light, well-drained soil and a sheltered position in full or light sun. The roots are vulnerable to severe frost: cover with straw in cold areas.

Renew plants every three or four years: in early or mid-spring, lift and divide roots, replanting young pieces 5–7.5cm/2–3in deep and 30–38cm/12–15in apart. It can also be raised from seeds, but plants raised in this way are said not to have such aromatic leaves. To encourage the development of leaves, pinch out flowering stems as soon as they appear.

HARVESTING

Use leaves fresh, picking them from early to late summer. Young shoots can also be cut and dried, although they soon lose their aroma. They can also be frozen.

USES

Apart from its use in tarragon vinegar, the leaves are a basic part of *fine herbes*, in the preparation of *sauce tartare* and French mustard. Leaves are also employed to flavour chicken and other white meats, as well as added to sauces, salads and fish dishes.

RUSSIAN ALTERNATIVE

*Russian Tarragon (*Artemisia dracunculus *'Indora'), is also known as False Tarragon and native to Southern Europe, Asia and North America west of the Mississippi River. It is hardier than the French type but does not have such a good flavour.*

Tarragon is a corruption of the French word meaning 'little dragon', relating to the days when Tarragon was thought to be a cure for the bites of these reptiles.

White flowers

Grey-green leaves

IN NORTH AMERICA, *Tarragon is also known as Estragona, a reference to a volatile oil extracted in France from the leaves and used in perfumery. It is also recommended as a cure for toothache.*

THYME
Thymus vulgaris

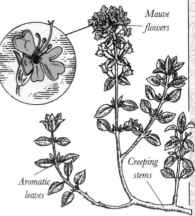

Mauve flowers

Creeping stems

Aromatic leaves

THE leaves of this hardy, aromatic, sprawling, evergreen shrub have been used to flavour food for many centuries. Their slightly spicy and sweet flavour has long been in demand. Indeed, this southern European herb was well known to the Greeks who called it 'thyme', a derivative of a word meaning to fumigate and thought to allude to its use as an incense or balsamic odour. Modern medicinal uses have drawn upon its age-old antiseptic qualities.

CULTIVATION
It grows 10–20cm/4–8in high, with narrow, dark green, aromatic leaves and clusters of tubular, mauve flowers in early summer.

Plant thyme in light, well-drained soil in full sun or light shade. Lift and divide plants in spring, every three or four years, replanting young pieces 23–30cm/9–12in apart.

Thyme can also be increased by forming sideshoots into 5–7.5cm/2–3in long cuttings in early summer. Preferably, they should have small pieces of the older wood still attached to their bases – known as heel-cuttings. Remove the lower leaves, trim the heel and insert about 2.5cm/1in deep in equal parts moist peat and sharp sand. Place in a cold frame and pot up individually into small pots.

HARVESTING
Pick off shoots and leaves when needed and use immediately. For drying, cut off stems about 15cm/6in long in late summer and tie into bunches of nine to twelve shoots. Hang up to dry. Leaves can also be frozen.

THYME *has for many centuries been used in kitchens, but it also has several medicinal qualities. In the seventeenth century the English physician and herbalist Nicholas Culpeper made an ointment from it to take away hot swellings and warts. Additionally it was used to ease sciatica, counteract dullness of sight and to take away pains.*

USES
Extensively employed in *bouquets garnis*, stuffings for rich meats, in soups and with fish, casseroles and other cooked dishes. It is often used mixed with other herbs and traditionally added to jugged hare.

LEMON THYME
*This decorative thyme (*Thymus x citriodorus*) is similar to normal thyme but with lemon-scented leaves and slightly larger flowers. It is used in a similar way to ordinary thyme, as well as included in* pot-pourri *and added to desserts.*

NOSEGAY GARDENS

EVEN the word nose-gay conjures thoughts of earlier years. It is said to have derived from the early English word *nose*, meaning fragrance, and *gay* implying toy or ornament. Now it means a bouquet or posy of redolent flowers and has come to encompass many aromatic herbs. Some of these herbs reveal fragrancies in their flowers, but others through their leaves. Scented posies are a delight in any room, introducing soothing and exciting scents throughout the year – especially welcome in winter.

RICH FRAGRANCES

One of the most popular and longest grown fragrant herbs is Rosemary, widely cultivated and spread throughout Europe by the Romans, since then acquiring many legends. Apart from being a shrub of remembrance and used in wedding and funeral services in France and England well into the nineteenth century, it was grown in kitchen gardens and came to represent the dominant influence in a house. This led to the once popular saying, *"Where Rosemary flourishes, the woman rules."*

Lavender grows wild and freely in Mediterranean regions, but some botanists consider it originated in India. Whatever its travels, it has been cultivated for many centuries. Initially, for medicinal reasons, claims were made that it comforted the brain. An elixir prepared during the seventeenth century, in which lavender was one of thirty herbs, was said to cure anything from swooning fits and barreness in women to vertigo and loss of memory.

Originally, lavender was grown in out-of-the-way clumps and not considered garden-worthy, but later, in the seventeenth century, Queen Henrietta Maria had a particular fondness for the white-flowered variety and it was used as an edging in knot-gardens. Dwarf varieties were

FOR *centuries, Lavender has been cultivated for its distinctive fragrance, which has been part of scented sachets.*

ROSEMARY *soon fills rooms with a rich, aromatic, slightly camphor-like aroma emitted from evergreen leaves. When cutting it for room decoration, hammer the stem ends flat and place overnight in water in a cool, still room.*

known as early as the sixteenth century – but not widely grown.

French Lavender (*Lavandula stoechas*) is more tender and less fragrant, but nevertheless well worth including in a scented herb garden. In England it was colloquially known as 'Cast-me-downe', a corruption of the earlier Cassidonie.

Thyme is another ancient plant and has a range of scents that will enrich nosegays and posies. The Mother of Thyme (*Thymus praecox)* has the well-known thyme-like bouquet, while others parade further exciting fragrancies. *Thymus x citriodorus* has a lemon redolence, *T. herba-barona* is more like caraway and *T. azoricus* is reminiscent of pine needles mixed with orange peel.

SCENTED ANNUALS

Nosegays and posies have a delicate, simple nature that encourages the use of scented plants cut from flower borders. Posies should not be packed with large, exotic flowers, but rather a kaleidoscope of simple, everyday plants. Many of these emit a sweet fragrance and none of these plants is more simple and popular than the Pot Marigold (*Calendula officinalis).* The Sweet Scabious (*Scabiosa atropurpurea)* has a warm, sweet and honeyed scent. The Sweet Mignonette (*Reseda odorata)* was made fashionable in

> SCENTED LEAVES
>
> *The range of plants with scented leaves is impressively large and includes spearmint and apple scents as well as many others. These include* Catmint (Nepeta x faassenii) *with mint-sauce scented leaves;* Lemon-scented Verbena (Lippia citriodora) *that reveals leaves especially redolent when gently bruised; and* the White Sage (Artemisia ludoviciana) *with a sweet and sage-like bouquet.*

CHAMOMILE (Anthemis nobilis) *develops finely-dissected, mid-green leaves that emit a refreshing aromatic bouquet. Daisy-like white flowers appear on short stems during summer. 'Treneague' has a banana-like aroma.*

France by the Empress Josephine, Napoleon being said to have returned in the 1790s from Egypt with it. As well as scenting nosegays, it was held in great esteem by lovers: legend suggest that success and good fortune will attend a lover who rolls in a bed of mignonette three times!

The nodding, bell-shaped flowers of Lily-of-the-Valley *(Convallaria majalis)* introduce a deliciously sweet and penetrating perfume to posies Earlier they were used to create Lily-of the-Valley water.

DISTILLING AND
EARLY MEDICINE

❖

PURIFYING and concentrating herbal mixtures has been performed for at least a couple of thousand years. It was the desire to separate the fragrant essence in rose water that led to distillation, first by the Greek physician Nicander in about 140 BC and later by the Alexandrians and Arabians. At that time, enormous quantities of rose water were used, both cosmetically and medicinally.

PERSIAN BEGINNINGS

The Persian empire was one of the cradles of pharmacy. Indeed, such was the development of pharmacy that in Sippara, on the Euphrates, in 1900 BC, the druggists lived in a separate street in accordance with ancient tradition.

From about 500 BC and during the next five hundred years, rational Greek medicine was to overshadow priestly and mystical attitudes, but this was to be eclipsed during the consolidation of the Roman Empire. The spread of Christianity and curing by 'mirac-

PERSIANS *were skilled herbalists and physicians. Here is a fifteenth century Persian Herbalist.*

───

DISTILLATION *is an ancient craft, developed by the Alexandrians and Arabians primarily to produce rose-water.*

ulous' medicine led to a decline in rational thinking. In AD 415 a fanatical Christian mob destroyed the medical school and library in Alexandria. The Christian church then continued to cure diseases by a mixture of faith and miracle-working. Plagues and pestilences were considered to be the wrath of God.

With the Arabian invasion in the seventh century, Greek science and medicine were reborn and within a century universities were built in Baghdad, Damascus and Cordova, as well as other places. Greek medical manuscripts were translated into Arabic, which became the universal language of learning and science. All of this expansion was aided by the manufacture of paper at Baghdad in AD 795, which replaced expensive parchment and papyrus.

THE OPIUM POPPY (Papaver somniferum) *was well known to the Romans as it is named after Somnus, the god of sleep. From it is derived one of the most powerful sleep-inducing narcotic drugs – opium. Morphine, an opium derivative, is named after Morpheus, the Greek god of dreams. While Heroin, a German trade-name for a form of morphine, was introduced into the medical world in 1898.*

EARLY DISTILLERS

By the end of the sixteenth century, distillation skills had developed and several alembic ovens built. Basically, these were vessels with beaked caps. An early form, an ambix, was described by the Greek physician Nicander in 140 BC. Here are are few alembic ovens from Mattioli's Commentaires *in 1579.*

PHYSIC GARDEN

❖

HYSIC gardens were repositories of medicinal herbs as well as centres where they were processed, stored and used. They were natural developments of work carried out in monasteries during the Dark Ages, when learning was less important than butchering people in foreign lands. In the later Middle Ages, the cultivation of herbs was take up by more nuns and monks, then slowly spreading. The uses of plants were refined and a better knowledge of them gained. Here are a few of them that were grown in the sixteenth century.

• Belladonna *(Atropa belladonna)* is the well-known Deadly Nightshade which produces the drug atropine. It gains its common name from the Italian *bella* meaning beautiful and *donna* for lady. During the Renaissance in Italy, ladies used atropine to beautify and enlarge the pupils of their eyes.

• Garlic *(Allium sativum)* was considered an all-embracing antiseptic and protection against the plague, as well as repelling demons and witches. Roman legions spread and ate the bulbs, believing it gave them courage in battle.

• The Yellow Gentian *(Gentiana lutea)*, also known as Gentian Root, has a bitter juice that was often used as a stomach tonic, cure for the plague and antidote against bites from snakes and mad dogs. A wine was also made from it in the eighteenth century and drunk as an apéritif before dinner.

• The Stinging Nettle *(Urtica dioica)* is a well known plant, spread by the Roman legions in their conquest of Europe. The soldiers are said to have been unhappy with the damp, cold, northerly weather and rubbed their limbs with nettle leaves to enliven their blood circulation. It also relieved rheumatism and toothache.

THE *Castor Oil Plant* (Ricinus communis) *has been cultivated since antiquity. Mainly grown for the oil which is expressed from the seed and used to relieve a wide range of complaints. The remains of the seed is highly poisonous.*

ABSINTH (Artemisia absinthium), *also known as Wormwood, was used to combat gout. It is fundamental in absinth, distilled from the dark green oil of this plant, mixed with Anise and said to be extremely intoxicating.*

HEMLOCK (Conium maculatum) *is a deadly plant and, although used medicinally for several thousand years, must be respected. Juice extracted from the roots provided the poison that killed Socrates, the Greek philosopher.*

IN THE *fifteenth and sixteenth centuries a sugar-coated medicinal sweet – known as a confect or comfit – was used as a household medicine and kept in a confection box. Good ones contained up to twelve different kinds of sugary pastilles. Here is a decorative lid from a sixteenth century confection box.*

• Corn Poppy *(Papaver rhoeas)*, also known as Red Poppy and Field Poppy, produces a syrup said to stop catarrhs and defluxions of the rheums from the head from flowing into the stomach and lungs.

• Black Mustard *(Brassica nigra)* has pungent seeds that since antiquity have been used medicinally: chewed they were said to eliminate toothache, swallowed they eased epilepsy, eliminated lethargy, cured stomach ache and cleansed the blood. When ground and sniffed they were said to purge the brain of sneezing! Additionally, when formed into a poultice, they eased swellings and reduced pain.

• The Common Paeony *(Paeonia officinalis)* has roots that when cleaned and infused produce a drink that would cure the falling sickness in old as well as young people. Additionally, the root or seed, when beaten into a powder and mixed with wine, was said to cleanse the womb after childbirth. And taken morning and night, the black seeds were used to remove melancholy dreams and troublesome nightmares.

• Common Henbane *(Hyoscyamus niger)* is a member of the nightshade family and extremely dangerous. It must never be taken internally. Indeed, it gains it name from the Anglo-Saxon *henn*, meaning chicken, and *bana* for murderer. Chickens and other fowls after eating the seeds are said to become paralysed and to die. The seeds are also poisonous to humans (especially children). Medically, henbane juice has been used as an antispasmodic, as a mouthwash for toothache and as drops for ear ache. Additionally, the leaves when applied as a warm fomentation are good for swellings of the testicles.

PHYSIC GARDENS *were full of activity during growing and harvesting times. Herbalist gave advice and directions, while early pharmacists processed the herbs and prepared them either for immediate use or storage. Some were distilled and others ground and powdered.*

PLANTS IN COSMETICS

❖

FROM ancient times, plants have been used in the making of cosmetics, and although it is likely that as a craft it originated in the East, the earliest records are in Egypt, where toilet articles were entombed with dead kings.

Cleopatra was noted for her beauty and charisma. At that time, embellishment of female eyes was important, the undersides being painted green and the lids, lashes and eyebrows black by the application of kohl, which was created from powdered antimony. Initially, painting eyes in this manner had been to protect them against strong sunlight.

Henna – derived from an Asian and North African shrub with leaves that produce an orange-red dye – was used by Egyptian women to paint nails, palms of hand and soles of feet. Persian women also used it.

Later, Italian women similarly made their eyes more noticeable, not with paint but a drug derived from Belladonna. Japanese women, by the way, used juices derived from the flowers of Rose of China *(Hibiscus rosa-sinensis)* to blacken their hair and eyebrows. Ultra-fashionable ladies of the Roman Court bleached their hair by means of a kind of soap that came from Gaul, while Ancient Britons used plant dyes, such as Woad, to colour their bodies. They were said by Romans to have frightening appearances!

For centuries, oriental women used the roots of the Snake's-head Iris (*Hermodactylus tuberosus* but earlier known as *Iris tuberosa*). First they were grated, then soaked in water. Women then rubbed it on their cheeks. Although it initially caused a tingling pain, it produced a lovely rosy hue which lasted for several days and withstood even a thorough scrubbing.

ATTRACTIVE CONTAINERS

The Romans created many attractive containers for cosmetics and perfumes, which could be arranged into three types: solid, liquid or powdered. The solid types were usually formed of one specific perfume, such as almond, rose or quince. Liquid types were usually compounds, formed of flowers, spices and gums, and immersed in either olive or sesame oil. Indeed, in the sixteenth century the Italian Marquis of Frangipani of Rome invented a creamy paste for scenting gloves, which were then very much in fashion.

In Britain, the return of knights from the Crusades introduced many toilet articles from the East. Toilet preparations were kept in 'sweet coffers' and considered to be essential furniture of bedrooms.

As early as 500 BC, women on the borders of the Black Sea pounded cedar wood, cypress and frankincense between stones, producing a powder they mixed with water and rubbed into their faces and bodies. It had a lovely scent and when removed left the skin pure and soft.

With the return to England of knights from the Crusades in eleventh, twelfth and thirteenth centuries, many Eastern sub-stances were intro-duced to women. These included perfumed oils, dyes for lips and eyes, and pastes to whiten the face. By the middle of the twelfth century, fashionable ladies were shaving the fronts of their heads, as well as parts of their eye-brows, to give themselves high foreheads. Unfortunately, this gave some  women a silly expres-sion, but one which they countered by using the Saffron Crocus to dye the remainder of their hair. By the time of Elizabeth I, in the six-teenth century, the custom was to whiten the face and neck, darken-ing the eyes and reddening and highlighting the cheeks.

The roots of anchusa have been used as rouge in many countries – Turkey, Persia, China, Russia, England and France. Additionally, it was employed by North American Indians to paint their bodies red. It was claimed that when used as rouge, anchusa has many advantages over other cos-metics: it lasted for many days and did not rub off. On the contrary, washing improved the shade and

it was certainly superior to the lead preparations which, unfortu-nately, sent many a seventeenth and eighteenth century woman to an early death.

Throughout histo-ry, women have used cosmetics to make themselves more attractive to men, but by the late  eighteenth century the English Parli-ament became so concerned about the amount and wide range of cosmetics used 'to entrap men into marriage' that an Act was passed imposing the same penal-ties as were then in force for the crime of witchcraft.

Throughout the centuries, men have also used cosmetics, and although the Spartans in Ancient Greece forbade colours and scents, the Athenians made a sci-ence of it. Indeed, there was a dif-ferent perfume for every part of the body: mint for use in armpits, palm oil for the chest, marjoram for hair and eyebrows, and crushed thyme for the knees and neck. It is even reported that top dogs in Greece had special oint-ments rubbed in their paws!

FEMALE *decoration has been pursued at least since the time of Egyptian ladies. Even the courtiers were decorated: in summer their nipples were painted gold.*

HERBS IN
FLOWER ARRANGING

❖

VASES *full of fresh, aromatic leaves and bright-faced flowers are a summer delight. Plants to consider include Pot Marigolds, Balm, mints and sages, Rosemary and Borage.*

Fresh herbs are ideal for creating unusual flower and foliage arrangements. Their sweet, old-fashioned, cool and refreshing fragrances make the display even more exciting. Be sure to put them in the right container, preferably one with an old, cool, white or lightly-patterned design. Avoid those with modern, brightly clinical designs, as well as those made of glass.

The choice of herbs is wide, but within each arrangement ensure that one of them is relatively large leaved and sufficiently dominant to hold the display together.

Here are some of the many herbs that create exciting displays.
• Balm (*Melissa officinalis*), with its lemon-scented, pale-green, somewhat heart-shaped leaves is ideal. However, do not fill the container with it. Rather, let it form the bones and shape of the design. Sprigs of Golden Balm (*Melissa officinalis* 'Aurea') are worth adding to the base of the arrangement.
• Pot Marigolds (*Calendula officinalis*) introduce bright, golden-orange beacons of colour to the arrangement. They look best when the design is positioned where it catches the last rays of evening sun. But as with all arrangements, do not place them in strong summer sunshine, as this dramatically reduces their life-span. This marigold, by the way, was earlier used medicinally to

1. CHOOSE *a rustic, wicker-work basket that harmonizes with the everyday nature of the flowers. Sides about 15cm/6in high help to create unity and to frame flowers and stems at the base of the display.*

2. PLACE *a large, heavy, earthenware container in the base of the basket. It does not matter if its rim is slightly higher than the basket's edge, as leaves and flowers will trail over and soften the edges.*

3. ARRANGE *the flowers and leaves so that there is a focal point to one end. Large flower heads and wispy stems of coloured leaves can be graduated downwards to a cluster of flowers at the front of the display.*

cure headaches, jaundice, red eyes and toothache. Additionally, the flowers were employed to give cheese a rich yellow shade.

• Nasturtiums (*Tropaeolum majus*) create a wonderfully informal display, with faintly-scented yellow or orange flowers. When crushed, the leaves have a pungent smell. Earlier, the flower buds and seeds were used as an alternative for capers, as well as to flavour vinegar. Allow the lax stems to trail over the sides of the container to soften its outline.

• Seed heads of all kinds introduce fresh shapes: herb gardens are often packed with attractive heads. In spring and early summer, hedge rows become alive with flower heads in the shape of umbrellas. Avoid the large ones, as they dominate arrangements.

• Mints and sages, especially those with variegated or coloured leaves, are worth including in limited amounts. The mints have an upward nature, while the leaves of sages cascade slightly and therefore are easier to unify with the rest of the display.

• Thymes, with their trailing stems, are ideal for softening the edges of vases. And, of course, their redolence makes them even more important.

• Borage (*Borago officinalis*), with its somewhat oval leaves covered with silvery hairs, helps to create a display with a refreshingly cool appearance. There are blue, white and pink-flowered forms.

• Rosemary (*Rosmarinus officinalis*) introduces permanency to arrangements, but sometimes is difficult to harmonize with the rest of the display. Unless the main theme of the display is Rosemary, use only small, delicate sprigs around the edges.

• Border plants with attractive, silvery leaves add a further dimen-

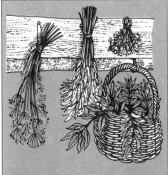

RUSTIC CUSTOMIZING

In cottage-type kitchens, few sights are more appealing and rural than bunches of herbs hanging to dry from ceilings. Dried flowers, seed-heads and grasses are other possibilities to customize your kitchen and to make it distinctive. These bunches can even be arranged to create a room-divider.

sion to arrangements. *Senecio bicolor* (earlier and better known as *Cineraria maritima*) has deeply-lobed, silvery leaves. For an even more casual look, use forms with deeply dissected leaves, such as 'Diamond' and 'Silver Dust'.

• Golden Privet *(ligustrum ovalifolium* 'Aureo-marginatum'), although not a herb, has a rural, simple and unpretentious appearance and is well worth adding, especially if it coincides with trimming hedges, (although sometimes it is also grown as a free-standing plant).

• Bergamot *(Monarda didyma)*, also known as Oswego Tea and Bee Balm, was used at one time to make a herbal tea. Its bright scarlet flowers create wonderful beacons of colour in flower borders as well as floral arrangements. It gains the name Oswego from a city on the shore of Lake Ontario in New York State.

HERBS IN POT-POURRI

❖

EW houses do not benefit from the fragrances of *pot-pourri*. Instead of relying on aerosols or pre-packed scented packages to refresh rooms, it is more interesting to create your own fragrancies. Few dogs do not offend human noses at sometime during the year with unappealing odours, while to many people cigarette smoke is even more objectionable. Sweet and penetrating scents soon suppress such smells and make homes more satisfying for residents as well as visitors.

TWO TYPES

Pot-pourri is a mixture of scented parts of plants: they can be 'moist' or 'dry' and both made at home, using garden or bought flowers. Spices and essential oils are available from specialist shops.

• <u>Moist *pot-pourris*</u> can be made throughout summer and usually retain their fragrance for several years. The only problem with them is their muddy-brown colour, which is not very attractive. They are therefore best covered. In earlier times, special con-

Rose for decoration

Essential oil

Rose petals

Cinnamon bark

Orris
(Iris germanica
'Florentina')

Cloves
(Eugenia
caryophyllus)

Nutmeg
(Myristica
fragrans)

Allspice
(Pimenta
dioica)

THE *range of perfume-yielding plants is wide. Some are tropical or subtropical, while others such as Lavender, Larkspur and Bay* grow quite easily in temperate climates. Indeed, pot-pourri *need not be expensive as many ingredients are readily available in* gardens. Leaves, flowers, seeds, berries as well as powdered bark and roots can create fragrant mixtures that will enhance your home.

tainers where made to hold them
and could be placed near a gently-
warm fire to warm up the mixture
to encourage the scent to escape.
When the room was filled with
fragrancies the lid was replaced
and the container moved to a cool
position to be rested.

There are many recipes for
moist *pot-pourri*: the one here
includes ingredients detailed on
the opposite page.

- *10 cups of partially dried rose petals*
  - *3 cups of coarse salt*
- *5 tablespoons powdered orris root*
  - *2 tablespoons ground allspice*
  - *2 tablespoons ground cinnamon*
  - *2 tablespoons ground nutmeg*
  - *1 tablespoon ground cloves*
  - *Few drops of essential oil,
    such as rose oil*
    ~

Preparation is easy: layer the salt
and petals in a large bowl and stir
daily. The salt will absorb moisture from the rose petals. When
intially added, they should have a
limp, soft but leathery texture. If
too dry they cannot be used in a
moist *pot-pourri* but can be added
to a dry type. It is also necessary
to 'press' the mixture to ensure
the layers are in close contact.
About three to six weeks later,
when the ingredients are dry,
crumble it and add the spices and
then the oil. Cover the mixture
and leave for several weeks to
'cure'. It can then be used. Place a
couple of dried roses on the surface for decoration.

- Dry *pot-pourri* is more attractive
and therefore can be left uncov-
ered in rooms. Because of this it
tends to lose its scent rather quickly, although fragrances can be
renewed by the further addition of
essential oils.

There are many recipes for dry
pot-pourri and they all can be modified to ensure that easily obtain-

SCENTED SACHETS

*These have been popular for
centuries for scenting closets,
drawers, blanket chests, beds,
sofas and pillows. Indeed, they
are used to create fragrancies
throughout the house.
Additionally, with silks and
elegant ribbons they can also be
made very elegant. Fill them with
mixtures of Lavender, Lemon
Verbena, rose petals and
chamomile flowers, as well as
Cloves, powdered Orris Root,
cedar shavings and essential oils.*

able plants are used. Here is the
basis of one recipe:

- *2 cups dried rose petals*
- *2 cups dried lavender flowers*
- *1 cup of cornflower petals to
  introduce colour*
- *1 cup lemon verbena leaves*
- *1/2 cup powdered orris root*
- *1 tablespoon ground allspice*
- *1 tablespoon ground cinnamon*
- *1 tablespoon ground cloves*
  few drops of essential rose oil
  ~

Mix all of these together and add
the essential oil until the fragrance
is strong enough. Put the entire
mixture in a large paper bag,
shake thoroughly and leave for
five to six weeks before placing in
attractive containers and putting
in rooms.

SOWING SEEDS

❖

THE majority of herbs are easily increased from seeds: most are sown outdoors in seed-beds, while a few are raised in greenhouses, sunrooms and conservatories to produce plants slightly earlier. Additionally, some, such as Parsley, can be grown indoors on window sills to produce leaves late in the year.

SOWING OUTDOORS

The times for sowing specific herbs is indicated on pages 16 to 39, but whatever the type there are certain requirements.

To prepare a seed-bed, from which young plants are later moved and planted into their growing positions, or where they are left after being thinned to grow, select a sheltered area away from cold winds. Additionally, the soil must be free from weeds, especially those with a pernicious perennial nature.

In winter, dig the area to about 30cm/12in deep and leave the surface rough. The action of frost, rain and wind will break down

---

ON WINDOWSILLS

Several herbs raised from seeds can be grown indoors on lightly-shaded window sills. These include:
- *Parsley* (Petroselinum crispum crispum)
- *Chervil* (Anthriscus cerefolium)
- *Summer Savory* (Satureja hortensis)
- *Sweet Basil* (Ocimum basilicum)

Clearly, some of these plants are quite tall on maturity and therefore once they outgrow the home they are best discarded.

---

large lumps of soil by the time spring arrives. About a week before sowing seeds, rake the surface level, at the same time further breaking down the soil.

If, however, the soil at raking-down time is still lumpy, use a garden fork to break it down. With a slightly sloping and

1. MANY *herbs can be increased from seeds. Fill a pot with loam-based or peat-based seed compost and firm it with your fingers around the edges. Fill it again, level and use the base of a small pot to firm it level.*

2. TIP *a few seeds into a piece of stiff, folded paper. Tap its edge to encourage seeds to fall evenly on the surface. Do not sow within 12mm/1/2in of the edges, as this is where drying often first occurs.*

3. USE *a sieve to lightly cover the seeds with finely-sieved compost. Horticultural sieves are available, but as a substitute a kitchen type can be bought and reserved for this use. Avoid damp compost.*

HERBS TO *raise outdoors include Angelica, Aniseed, Balm, Borage, Caraway, Chervil, Chives, Coriander, Dill, Fennel, French Sorrel, Hyssop and Savory. Some, such as Parsley, Sweet Basil and Sweet Marjoram, can be raised in greenhouses as well as in gardens.*

Fennel

Caraway

Hyssop

Angelica

sideways-dragging motion, hit the surface so that the four tines touch the surface simultaneously. Then, use a rake.

Tread over the complete surface uniformly, using a sideways shuffling motion. Do not use a roller, as this invariably consolidates one area more than another, and in any case is too heavy. Then rake the surface level.

Use a draw-hoe to form shallow drills – and either a garden line or a straight-edged board as guidance to ensure the drill is straight. Sow seeds evenly and thinly. When the drill has been sown, use the back of a rake to pull soil over the seeds. Alternatively, straddle the row and shuffle along with your feet in a V-shape. Afterwards, walk along the row to consolidate the soil. Lightly rake along the direction of the row to level the surface. Do not rake across it, as this may disturb some seeds.

SOWING IN POTS

Herbs such as Parsley, Sweet Basil and Sweet Marjoram can be sown in greenhouses. The method for sowing these seeds is illustrated and described below, with specific details of temperatures and times on pages 16 to 39.

4. WATER *the compost by standing the pot in a saucer of clean water. When moisture seeps to the surface, remove and allow to drain. Do not water the compost from above, as the seeds will then be washed about.*

WHEN *the seedlings are large enough to handle, transfer them to seed-trays or pots. Later, they are usually planted into a herb garden outdoors. Some, such as Parsley, are moved into other pots and grown on window sills indoors.*

TAKING CUTTINGS

❖

 SEVERAL herbs are increased by taking cuttings from them. The majority of these have a permanent nature, such as Bay and Rosemary, while Pot Marjoram is a bushy, low-growing shrub with soft stems but a woody base, especially when aged.

Cuttings from soft-stemmed herbs, such as Pot Marjoram, initially need gentle warmth and cosseting, while those from Bay, which have a woody nature, are hardier and can be increased without the need of greenhouse warmth. Indeed, cuttings from Rosemary develop roots quite easily in pots containing equal parts moist peat and sharp sand, then placed on a sheltered, lightly-shaded patio. By the following spring they will have rooted and can be planted into a herb garden or tubs. Clearly, however, in extremely cold regions this is not possible and a garden frame or cold greenhouse is needed to give winter protection.

VINEGAR OF THE FOUR THIEVES

Rue has been famed since early times for warding off contagious diseases and preventing attacks from fleas and other noxious insects. But is was also an ingredient of a concoction known as the Vinegar of the Four Thieves, used by thieves in Marseilles to enter and rob homes stricken with plague. It also formed part of an ale against the plague. In the sixteenth and seventeenth centuries it was used in Law Courts to protect judges from jail-fever.

ROOT CUTTINGS

Only a few herbs are increased in this way, Horseradish being the notable one. However, the tropical spices Ginger *(Zingiber officinale)* and Turmeric *(Curcuma longa)* have rhizomes, which both provide the spices and the way to increase

1. POT MARJORAM (Origanum onites) *is easily increased from soft-wood cuttings. The day before severing the cuttings, thoroughly water the mother plant to ensure they will not wilt. Sever long shoots cleanly at the plant's base.*

2. TRIM *each cutting 5-7.5cm/2-3in long, severing below a leaf joint and cutting the lower leaves close to the stem. Always used a sharp knife to avoid leaving ragged ends – these delay healing and the development of roots.*

3. FILL *a pot with equal parts moist peat and sharp sand, firming it to within 12mm/1/2in of the rim. Use a dibber to form holes – about 12mm/1/2in from the pot's side – and insert a cutting in each one. Firm compost around them.*

SEVERAL herbs can be increased from cuttings, including Bay, Hyssop, Spearmint, Rue, Sage and Pot Marjoram. The times to take and insert cuttings of these plants is described on pages 16 to 39. Some are softwood cuttings, such as Pot Marjoram, while others like Bay are semi-ripe heel-cuttings. They are formed during mid- to late summer.

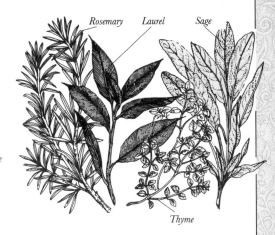

Rosemary   Laurel   Sage

Thyme

them. The fat, firm, underground stems are divided at planting time.

• Ginger is used to flavour foods in many countries, and an important flavouring in curry powder. It is also used in making ginger beer.

• Turmeric is a major ingredient of curry powders, imparting a bright yellow colour as well as a rich, spicy flavour.

• Liquorice (*Glycyrrhiza glabra*) is less tender, well-known to the ancient Greeks and grown in the British Isles since the sixteenth century. The liquorice gained from the roots was used in Pontefract Cakes. The rhizomes and roots often reach 1.2m/4ft deep, with a similar spread. These are ground into a pulp and boiled in water, the extract then concentrated by evaporation. Division of the roots is one of the ways in which it is increased.

• Horseradish is a member of the wallflower family and said to be one of the bitter herbs eaten by Jews during the feast of the Passover. The thong-like roots form cuttings (see page 28).

4. GENTLY *water the cuttings to settle compost around their bases. Allow excessive water to drain, then place in a warm, lightly shaded place until they are rooted. Then, remove the cuttings and carefully transfer into larger pots.*

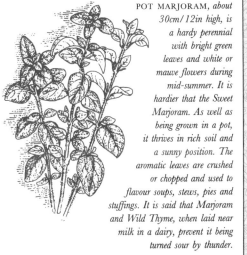

POT MARJORAM, *about 30cm/12in high, is a hardy perennial with bright green leaves and white or mauve flowers during mid-summer. It is hardier that the Sweet Marjoram. As well as being grown in a pot, it thrives in rich soil and a sunny position. The aromatic leaves are crushed or chopped and used to flavour soups, stews, pies and stuffings. It is said that Marjoram and Wild Thyme, when laid near milk in a dairy, prevent it being turned sour by thunder.*

DIVIDING HERBS

❖

F ALL the ways to increase herbs, division is the quickest method to produce established plants. Congested plants – in pots or growing in a herb garden – can be separated into smaller pieces, discarding old, central parts and retaining only the young and outer pieces.

Dividing herbs established in pots is illustrated and described below. These include Chives, which can be taken indoors and grown on kitchen window sills to produce leaves out of their normal season. Others, such as mint, are so invasive and vigorous that it is necessary to constrain them in pots on a patio or in bottomless buckets in herb borders.

DIVIDING
ESTABLISHED CLUMPS

Autumn or early spring are the best times to lift and divide congested plants. If the soil is moist there is no need to water the clump within the previous twenty-four hours. But if the season is dry, thoroughly water the plants as well as the area into which they are to be planted. However, avoid making the soil too wet and turning the area into a bog.

Use a garden fork to dig under a congested clump and place it on a large sack or piece of hessian. Do not contaminate lawns, paths or gravel chippings with soil. Usually, congested herbs can be pulled apart by hand. Discard old, central parts and retain only young pieces from around the outside. Do not divide them excessively: if too small, they do not create an attractive display within a reasonable time.

Before planting them, fork over the border and add a general fertilizer. Firm it slightly before setting the new plants in position. If space allows, always use three plants of the same type. Used singly or just in twos, they either look sparse or imbalanced. Three or five are the magical numbers to success when setting any plants in a border.

1. WATER *the clump the day before separating it. Invert the pot, place a hand under the root-ball and tap the rim on a firm surface. If the ball of roots remains in the pot, run a knife between the soil-ball and pot.*

2. GENTLY *but firmly pull the tangled roots into several pieces. Do not make these too small: it is better to have a few large clumps than many thin and weedy-looking ones. Discard old, central parts. Use only young, outer pieces.*

3. FILL *a small pot with compost and pot up the pieces individually. Repot each piece to the same depth as before, leaving about 12mm/¹/2in between the surface and the pot's rim. Water from above.*

DIVISION *is the most assured way to increase herbs. The types that can be increased in this way include Balm, Chives, French Sorrel, French Tarragon and Spearmint. Additionally, the many other types of mint are easily increased in the same way, as well as by cuttings. These include Peppermint (*Mentha x piperita*), AppleMint (*Mentha rotundifolia *but also known as* M. suaveolens).*

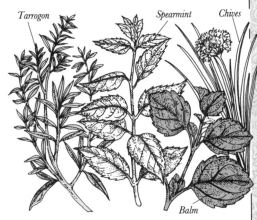

Tarrogon   Spearmint   Chives

Balm

Spread out the young plants on the surface of the border. It is then possible to stand back and view the arrangement from several aspects before deciding on their exact positions. If the whole herb border is being replanted and freshly dug, replanting is often delayed: keep the roots of the plants damp during this period by wrapping them in wet newspaper or sacking. If the microscopic root-hairs become dry and badly damaged, it takes much longer for a plant to become established when planted. Indeed, if roots become very dry the plants will never recover.

Some plants naturally have 'face' sides: angles from which they are the most attractive. Ensure these aspects face the front of a border. Use a trowel to take out a hole large enough to accommodate the roots. Spread them out and cover with friable soil, firming it gently but firmly.

After planting, use an edge of a trowel to level the surface, then water the plants thoroughly but gently. Then, lightly water the compost to settle it down around the roots.

HANDSOME FAMILY

Like mints, the sages also have a prolific and attractive range. Some are exceptionally decorative. They are ideal for planting a garden border.

- *'Albiflora': Handsome, white flowers. Said to be a superb culinary sage.*
- *'Aurea' (Golden Sage): Green and gold leaves. Plants have a compact habit.*
- *'Icterina': Sometimes known as 'Variegata', it is exceptionally attractive, with grey-green leaves variegated with yellow. It is ideal for planting in flower borders as well as herb gardens.*
- *'Purpurascens' (Purple-leaf Sage): Stems and leaves suffused greyish-purple. It is thought to be the Red Sage known in the sixteenth century.*
- *'Purpurascens Variegata': Leaves attractively variegated with greyish-purple.*
- *'Tricolor': Leaves variegated white and often edged or tipped with purple. Raised in France about a hundred years ago, probably a sport of the Purple-leaf Sage.*

PESTS AND DISEASES

❖

HERBS, like all other plants, are susceptible to attack from pests and diseases, especially soft stems and leaves. Also, herbs at the seedling stage in greenhouses, sunrooms and conservatories are likely to be attacked by damping-off and other greenhouse problems. Outdoors, soil pests such as cutworms and wireworms are a problem, as well as general types like woodlice, earwigs, snails, caterpillars and slugs.

Always use chemicals suitable for edible crops and check the period recommended between spraying and eating. Additionally, never experiment with a chemical's strength – it is wasteful and could be dangerous. Always adhere to the manufacturer's instructions and thoroughly wash equipment after use.

GREENFLY (APHIDS) *suck sap, causing mottling and distortion. Because herbs are added to food, take care when spraying and dusting them and use only chemicals recommended for use on edible crops.*

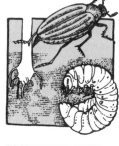

COCKCHAFER GRUBS *live in garden soil and graze on the roots of plants. Later they pupate and beetles appear. Pick up and destroy the grubs; dig new herb borders deeply in winter and dust with gamma-HCH.*

CATERPILLARS *chew soft leaves and stems, quickly decimating plants. Pick them off and spray with an insecticide suitable for edible crops. Clear away and burn all rubbish in winter to reduce their spread.*

CUTWORMS, *the larvae of certain moths, chew seedlings and young plants at soil level, causing them to collapse. Dust the soil with gamma-HCH and hoe soil regularly.*

DAMPING-OFF *is a disease of seedlings in greenhouses and caused by high humidity, and badly drained compost. Water the compost with a fungicide and avoid high temperatures.*

EARWIGS *are pernicious pests, especially eating soft stems, leaves and flowers. Pick off and destroy, trap in inverted pots packed with straw, or spray or dust with a pesticide.*

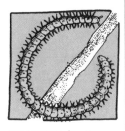

FLEA BEETLES *chew roundish holes in seedlings and young leaves and are especially active on sunny days in the late spring. Spray carefully with derris or dust with gamma-HCH.*

GREY-MOULD *(botrytis) is a fungal disease that enters plants through cuts and wounds. Encouraged by damp, still air. Remove infected tissue and spray with a fungicide.*

MILLIPEDES *have two pairs of legs on each body segment and are slower moving than centipedes. They chew seedlings, bulbs, young roots and tubers. Dust with a pesticide.*

MINT RUST *is pernicious, first appearing in spring and causing orange, later black, pustule-like spores on stems. Burn seriously infected plants, buy healthy stock and plant into fresh soil.*

SLUGS *are ravenous chewers of plants, especially soft stems and leaves. Also, they leave unsightly trails of slime over plants. Use slug baits, but ensure they are not accessible to domestic pets.*

SNAILS *are similarly destructive to slugs and very familiar to gardeners, especially during warm, wet seasons. Control them in a similar way to that used for slugs. They decimate plants.*

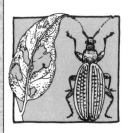

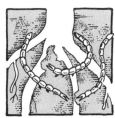

WEEVILS *are beetle-like and often have long, divided snouts. Their larvae are leg-less grubs. Both adults and larvae feed on roots, stems and leaves. Regularly dust or spray with insecticide.*

WIREWORMS *are the larvae of click-beetles, which eat roots, stems, bulbs and tubers. They are especially prevalent in newly-cultivated land. Use insecticides and hoe the soil regularly.*

WOODLICE *are hard-coated pests living in damp, dark places. They come out at night and feed on stems, roots and leaves. Dust with gamma-HCH and keep the area free from rubbish.*

HERB CALENDAR

❖

Numbers in brackets are page references.

SPRING

This is the main season of regeneration in herb gardens, when plants are increased.

IN THE GREENHOUSE

- Sow Sweet Basil in 13°C/55°F in early spring (19)
- Sow Sweet Marjoram in late winter or early spring in 13– 15°C/55–59°F (30)

IN THE GARDEN

- Sow Angelica in seed-beds in late spring or early summer (16)
- In early to mid-spring, plant Angelica (16)
- Sow Aniseed in mid-spring (17)
- Divide congested Balm plants in autumn or spring (18)
- Sow Balm spring (18)
- Sow Sweet Basil during late spring (19)
- Sow Borage from mid-spring to mid-summer (21)
- Sow Chervil from late spring to mid-summer (23)
- Sow Chives in spring or early summer (24)
- Sow Coriander during early spring (25)
- Sow Dill from early spring to mid-summer (26)
- Sow Fennel from late spring to early summer (27)
- Sow Hyssop during mid- and late spring (29)
- Take cuttings of Hyssop in late spring (29)
- Sow Sweet Marjoram during mid- and late spring (30)
- Divide Mint (31)
- Sow Parsley in spring (32)
- Cut out dead shoots of Rosemary in early spring (33)
- Sow both Summer and Winter Savory in mid-spring (36)
- Divide French Tarragon in spring (38)

SUMMER

Early summer is still a time for sowing seeds of many herbs. Also, there are cuttings to be taken.

IN THE GREENHOUSE

- Take cuttings of Bay during mid- to late summer, placing them in a greenhouse or cold frame (20)

IN THE GARDEN

- Pick herbs when young and fresh for freezing (14-15)
- Pick seed-heads for drying and storing (14-15)
- Ensure you have a stock of clean, airtight jars (14-15)
- Ensure a supply of ice-cube trays, plastic bags, labels and twist ready for liquid freezing herbs (14-15)
- Sow Angelica seeds in seed-beds in late spring or summer (16)
- Trim Bay trees in large tubs several times in summer (20)
- Sow Borage from mid-spring to mid-summer (21)
- Sow Caraway during late summer (22)
- Sow Chervil from late spring to mid-summer (23)
- Sow Chives in spring or early summer (24)
- Sow Dill from early spring to mid-summer (26)
- Sow Fennel from late spring to early summer (27)
- Take cuttings of Mint (31)
- Sow Parsley in summer (32)
- Take cuttings of Rue in mid-summer (34)
- Take cuttings of Rosemary in mid-summer (33)
- Take cuttings of Sage in late summer (35)
- Sow Sorrel in mid-summer (37)
- Take cuttings of Thyme in early summer (39)

AUTUMN

This is a season of clearing up and ensuring the herb garden is clean and tidy. Annual herbs will be dying down and these need to be cleared away. Cut down the stems of herbaceous herbs and put them on a compost heap. If very woody, burn them. It is essential to clear away all rubbish as if left it encourages the presence of pests and diseases (see pages 58-9).

Biennial herbs are either transplanted to their main growing positions now or, if the weather is very cold, in spring.

Late autumn is a time for review and decisions about creating a new herb garden or replanting the present one. Sketch out on graph paper a design that fits the area to be devoted to it. An out line for a cart-wheel herb garden is given on pages 10 and 11. There is also the possibility of growing herbs in containers on a patio or balcony.

Many specialist herb nurseries issue catalogues of established plants they offer, while seed companies have comprehensive lists. Gather a few of these and plan your order well in advance of spring to ensure you are not to be disappointed later.

IN THE GREENHOUSE
- In cold areas, cuttings of Bay, Rosemary and Rue need the protection of cloches, garden frames or cold greenhouses during autumn and throughout winter. Wet autumns and winters can be just as damaging as low temperatures – a combination of both is lethal.

IN THE GARDEN
- Divide congested Balm plants in autumn or spring (18)
- In autumn or early winter, cut down Balm plants (18)

WINTER

At the peak of winter there is little to do in a herb garden but to contemplate better weather and the onset of spring. The exact time when the weather improves depends on the locality and latitude. It is worth keeping a diary of weather dates – first and last frost as well as lowest and highest temperatures.

During winter, take care when clearing away snow and ice from natural stone paths where small herbs are growing between the paving slabs. Do not used a spade to move snow, neither spread salt on the path to free it of ice. Also, do not use ashes to provide a better grip for shoes.

All these methods soon kill plants. Indeed, using salt may not only destroy the present plants but make the immediate area unfit for plants for several seasons.

IN THE GREENHOUSE
- Sow Sweet Marjoram in late winter or early spring in 13–15°C/55–59°F (30)
- Sow Parsley in 10–15°C/ 50–59°F in late winter (32)

IN THE GARDEN
- Prepare a new herb garden by digging the soil to the depth of a spade. It helps to control soil-pests (58-9). While digging, remove all weeds, especially those of perennial types. Some, like Couch Grass and Horse's Tail, if chopped up become even more of a problem. Therefore, ensure all pieces of them are removed and burned.
- In autumn or early winter, cut down Balm plants (18)
- In early winter, dig up Horseradish plants and cut up the roots (28). These are later formed into cuttings.

USEFUL HERB TERMS
❖

AIR DRYING: *A method of drying herbs so that they can be stored and used when not available in a fresh form.*

ALEMBIC: *An early method of distilling and basically a vessel with a beaked cap.*

AMBIX: *A Greek term, meaning a cup with a stem. Perhaps the earliest example of distilling equipment.*

ANNUAL: *A plant that grows from seed, flowers and dies within the same year. Many herbs are raised in this way.*

APOTHECARY: *A person who prepares and sells drugs and medicines.*

BIENNIAL: *A plant that grows from seed, making its initial growth one year and flowering during the following one.*

BLANCH: *Sometimes used to help herbs retain their colour prior to drying. Involves quickly dipping them in boiling water for a few seconds.*

BOLTING: *A plant that prematurely develops seeds, rather than continuing normal growth. Usually caused by drought, hot weather or exceptionally poor soil conditions.*

BOUQUET GARNI *(pl.* bouquets garnis*): A bunch of herbs, tied together or wrapped in cheesecloth. Used as seasoning in cookery.*

CART-WHEEL HERB GARDENS: *An arrangement of herbs, as if planted between the spokes of a large wheel. If a wheel is not available, stones can be used to form the spokes and rim, with a large herb such as Bay planted in the centre.*

CLOVE: *A segment of a garlic bulb.*

COMFIT: *A sugarcoated sweet, initially a way to dispense herbal medicines.*

CONFECT: *Originally, a sweet confection, a comfit.*

CONFECTION BOX: *Earlier, a box holding comfit and performing the role of a modern medicine cabinet.*

CULPEPER, NICHOLAS: *Famous English herbalist and physician (1616–54) who wrote* The English Physician, *which later became better known as his* Herbal.

CULINARY: *Relating to cooking and the kitchen.*

DIBBER: *Pencil-like rod with a rounded end. Use to transfer seedlings and to insert cuttings in compost.*

DRUGGIST: *One who sells and dispenses drugs and medicines (mainly an American term).*

ESSENTIAL OIL: *A volatile oil, usually having the characteristic odour of the plant from which it is derived, and used to make perfumes and flavourings.*

FINES HERBES: *A French term for finely-chopped herbs, such as Chives, Parsley, Thyme, Tarragon. Used as a seasoning.*

FLORAL WATERS: *Distilled water to which is added various scented flowers or petals.*

FREEZING HERBS: *Method of making herbs available for cookery out of their normal season, usually during winter but as a convenience throughout the entire year.*

FREEZING WHOLE: *When entire sprigs or shoots are frozen. They are packed in plastic bags and placed in a freezer.*

FREEZING IN WATER: *Leaves removed from stems, chopped finely, placed in ice-cube compartments, water added then frozen. They are best used in soups and stews.*

FRUIT CUP: *A non-alcoholic drink made from mixed fruit juices. Fresh herbs are also added to them.*

GARNISH: *Using herbs, either whole or chopped, to enhance the appearance of food and to add flavouring.*

GERALD, JOHN: *Famous English herbalist (1545–1612) who wrote* The Herball or General Historie of Plants. *It was later revised by Thomas Johnson in 1633, correcting many of the earlier mistakes.*

HARDEN OFF: *Acclimatize plants to outdoor conditions. Usually applies to plants raised in greenhouses, sunrooms and conservatories in late winter or early spring.*

HEEL CUTTING: *A method of increasing woody plants, including some herbs. Part of an older shoot is left attached to the base of each cutting.*

HERBACEOUS: *A plant that dies down to ground level in autumn or early winter and develops fresh shoots in spring.*

HERBAL: *A book containing the names and descriptions of herbs, their properties and uses.*

HERBAL TEA: *An infusion of one or more herbs. Usually forms a medicinal drink.*

MAITRE D'HOTEL: *A sauce of melted butted, chopped Parsley, lemon juice, pepper and salt.*

MEDICINAL: *Having curative and healing powers. Derived from roots, stems, leaves and flowers.*

NOSEGAYS: *An early term for a bunch of fragrant, attractive flowers.*

OVEN-DRYING: *A method of drying herbs to make them available out of their normal season.*

PARKINSON, JOHN: *Famous English herbalist (1576–1650) who wrote* Theatrum Botanicum.

PERFUMED PAPERS: *Writing papers made more attractive and pleasant to use by scenting them with herbs like Lavender and Rosemary.*

PHARMACY: *The science of preparing and dispensing drugs, or a place where drugs are dispensed.*

PHARMACOPOEIA *(also, pharmacopeia):* *A book containing an official list of medicinal drugs, together with information about their preparation and use.*

PHYSIC GARDEN: *A area devoted to growing medicinal plants.*

PHYSICK GARDEN: *An earlier name for physic garden, when it was part of a monastery garden.*

POMANDER: *A mixture of aromatic substances in an apple-shaped container. Formerly regarded as a protection against infection. Nowadays, it is used to perfume rooms.*

POSY *(pl. posies):* *A small bunch of flowers, usually fragrant. A more recent term for nosegay.*

POT-POURRI *(pl.* pot-pourris): *A mixture of petals and spices kept in a jar and used to scent the air. Some* pot-pourris *are 'moist', others 'dry'. Moist types tend to look a muddy brown and therefore are best kept covered. Dry types are more decorative but tend to lose their scent more quickly, although this can be revived by using an essential oil.*

PRICKING OFF: *The initial moving of seedlings from where they were sown into pots or seed-trays.*

PUREE: *To convert vegetables, roots or fruits into a semi-solid state.*

ROOT-CUTTINGS: *Method of propagating plants, such as the culinary herb Horseradish.*

ROSE-WATER: *A fragrant preparation made by steeping or distilling rose petals in water. Used both cosmetically and medicinally.*

SACHET: *Small bag or packet containing perfumed herbs. Used to scent clothes, especially in drawers, trunks and wardrobes.*

SAUCE TARTARE *see* TARTARE SAUCE

SELF-SOWN SEEDLINGS: *Seedlings that occur naturally around plants from ripe seeds shed by them.*

SWEET COFFERS: *A chest in which toiletries were kept. Originally used in the eleventh, twelfth and thirteenth centuries by ladies in their bedrooms.*

TARTARE SAUCE *(also,* sauce tartare *and tartar sauce):* *Sauce formed of mayonnaise mixed with chopped onions, Chives, pickles and capers, and served as a sauce with fish.*

THINNING: *Removing congested seedlings to leave healthy ones spaced out.*

POCKET GARDENING GUIDES

INDEX